best-loved

plants

best-loved
plants

MARGARET CROWTHER,
SUE HOOK & DAVID SQUIRE

PaRragon

Bath New York Singapore Hong Kong Cologne Delhi Melbourne

This edition published in 2008

Parragon
Queen Street House
4 Queen Street
Bath BA1 1HE, UK

Produced by The Bridgewater Book Company Ltd.

ISBN: 978-1-4054-6378-2

Printed in China

NOTE

For growing and harvesting, calendar information applies
only to the Northern Hemisphere (US zones 5–9).

contents

introduction

Gardening is a stimulating and rewarding hobby and there is a deep sense of satisfaction in creating an attractive garden. Part of this success derives from choosing a style that especially appeals to you and your family and these range from cottage gardens to those with a Mediterranean nature. Other types include traditional English gardens with borders burgeoning with herbaceous

▼ *The geometric lines of this herb garden are softened as the many different varieties begin to grow and billow out.*

perennials, scented gardens, rock and water gardens and, of course, borders and walls packed with roses. There is even the possibility of creating a Japanese garden. Some gardeners – and especially those with only a small garden – have a preference for a patio, courtyard or terrace area, where plants in containers give a concentrated display. Additionally, there is often a desire for seasonal displays, such as those which are at their best during spring and summer. Winter displays, however, also have attractive qualities and are much in demand by

gardeners who admire frost patterns on grass and plants, as well as distinctive flowers such as the yellow, spider-like ones on *Hamamelis japonica*, the Japanese Witch Hazel. This book is packed with information about plants, styles of gardening and seasonal gardens, while the all-embracing plant directory creates a parade of plants that will ensure the right plants are always selected.

Gardening in containers

Many plants can be grown in containers on a patio or terrace, where they create

◀ *This minimalist garden employs strong hard-landscaping and design features. Perfect for a low-maintenance garden.*

▼ *Many different materials can link the garden to the home – reclaimed railway sleepers and gravel are good for steps.*

either a seasonal or permanent display. Summer-flowering bedding plants bought in late spring or early summer create a kaleidoscope of colour right through until autumn. Small conifers in tubs and large pots will enrich your garden with interesting shapes and colours throughout the year, while many shrubs have either beautiful leaves or flowers. Additionally, there are some, such as the yellow-leaved Mexican Orange Blossom (*Choisya ternata* 'Sundance'), with both attractive leaves and beautiful flowers. And with this evergreen shrub there is the bonus of an unusual fragrance.

As well as decorating a garden at ground level, several types of container can be used to bring brightness to walls. Window boxes are ideal for decorating windowsills, while wall baskets and mangers can be used to make bland areas more attractive. Hanging baskets full of trailing plants are superb for decorating the sides of entrances, as well as walls.

Additionally, they can be used to cloak unsightly drain pipes.

Old stone sinks are popular and when placed on four bricks create ideal homes on patios for small rock garden plants, from miniature conifers and dwarf shrubs to true alpines. Miniature bulbs such as *Crocus chrysanthus*, *Narcissus cyclamineus* and *N. bulbocodium* are also good choices. In addition to old stone sinks, which can be expensive, glazed sinks can be modified to create attractive homes for rock garden plants.

Vegetable and herb gardening

To many gardeners the epitome of good gardening is growing your own vegetables and culinary herbs. Usually, large vegetable plots are needed, but a few vegetables can be grown in small areas and especially with the benefit of large pots and growing-bags. Culinary herbs are easy to grow and many are ideal for planting in pots and planters.

Where bending is a problem, pots of herbs can be positioned on the tops of firm, wide walls or a specially constructed framework; in addition to making them more accessible it helps to prevent slugs and snails eating the plants. However, the compost in the pots is likely to become dry more rapidly than when at ground level.

gardening styles

There are styles of gardening to please everyone, from traditional borders packed with herbaceous perennials, bulbs, shrubs and small trees to meadow gardens and the nostalgic nature of cottage gardens. Scented borders and those that are at their best during evenings and at night are also possible, as well as Mediterranean, Japanese and Zen gardens. Richly coloured rose gardens are always welcome, while flower arrangers appreciate borders and corners that yield flowers and leaves for arranging indoors.

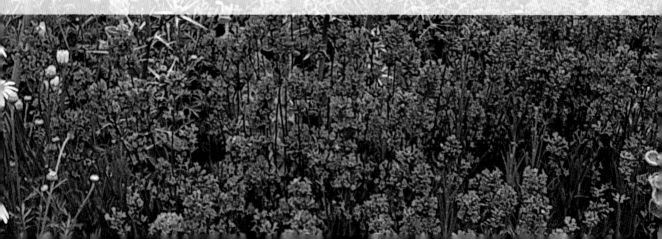

border gardens

The border, with its blend of colour and mix of heights and shapes, is a true garden classic, even though in fact it is really a twentieth-century creation. Just about any garden in any situation can become a border garden – generous paths and deep beds are key ingredients for successful design.

The mixed border

The traditional lush border on a grand scale was at its best in high summer but today's more relaxed planting and the continual introduction of new plants means that the whole garden can be used for borders which have something to offer all year round. While borders in the past consisted of perennials and seasonal bedding plants, today they incorporate climbers, small trees, deciduous and evergreen shrubs, spring- and autumn-flowering bulbs, and annuals too.

Perennials still form the mainstay of a border, but the general mix ensures there is something of interest from shape and colour at almost any time of year. The spring bulbs and early summer annuals bring life and colour before the high-summer perennials are at their best. Height is supplied by climbers, and shape, form and long-term structure are derived from evergreens, trees and larger shrubs, to make a harmonious whole allowing the colour to be seen within a framework.

Most gardens have a sunny and shady aspect and you can take advantage of this to create two borders with very different characters. Hot borders have caught the contemporary imagination. Flowers and foliage with a high intensity of colour

◀ *A modern mixed border uses shrubs, perennials and grasses to create continued colour, shape and texture throughout the year.*

▶ *This border relies for much of its effect on the interplay of contrasting leaf shapes and shades of green foliage as a foil to the flowers.*

are the first ingredient, but second is the way they are mixed, in what would once have been considered 'clashes', such as deep carmine, orange and purple with blue. Most of the plants for hot borders are not just stunningly bright colours by accident, they also signal their preference for sun this way. They tend also to offer strong, spiky forms. On the shady side colour can be gentle, with white and blue, cream, lilac or pale pink, and shapes may be softer too. Dark green from evergreens, and light green border plants, such as alchemilla, will help tie the scheme together.

Essentials

Although the complete effect is important, part of the pleasure of a border garden is the way it leads the eye and allows the foot to follow, so that not all of it is seen at once, and there is always more to discover from a different viewpoint. Curving beds help to create this effect in even the smallest garden. If you can contrive to make the gap between the borders wide at the beginning and narrow at the end this heightens perspective.

Paths and walkways are an essential part of the scheme and you also need somewhere finally to sit and admire the whole thing after inspecting the beds in close-up, if possible at the far end, away

◀ *Pots allow you to plug gaps in borders so you need never see bare earth patches. Try a variety of materials such as terracotta and metal.*

from the house. When using curves, try to make them generously sweeping, not tight and contorted. When two borders face each other in complementary curves with an open area between them they can be enjoyed from many different angles. This helps to give the garden a feeling of greater size too, as you can't take everything in at once and there is more to be revealed round the bend.

Between the beds areas of lawn are traditional, and they are the perfect foil. In a dry garden where grass would need constant attention, gravel or stone can pay a pleasing compliment to the softening effect of flowering plants. The background completes the whole. Of course the ideal traditional border is backed by a yew hedge but this takes space and absorbs nutrients the border plants would be glad to get their roots on. In a small garden, trellis with climbing plants may be better.

cottage gardens

A cottage garden doesn't have to be in the country, but a small plot with a compact design is a key ingredient. In a cottage garden vegetables, flowers and fruits are jumbled up together so that the effect is of a haze of myriad colours, textures and scents with plants allowed to self-seed at random.

◄ *In a cottage garden a wide range of plants — from flowers and herbs to fruits and vegetables — are grown closely together.*

An idyll from the past

The real cottage garden of old was far removed from our romantic visions of today in which flowering plants loll over winding paths attracting bees and butterflies; for the plot around a cottage in the past had to be put to good use. Plants were grown for food, for medicine and for practical purposes such as dyeing and keeping away fleas and lice or scenting household linen to disguise the smell of mildew. Flowering plants on the whole had a practical function as well as providing visual delight. The crammed appearance of the garden resulted from the need to get as much use as possible out of a small plot.

Modern cottage gardeners can adapt this idea by growing a variety of fruits, herbs and vegetables among the flowers and by making use of every bit of space, including the vertical. The look is not for those who prefer order. In it plants jostle against their neighbours with not a patch of bare earth in sight. Informality is the key to this style. The would-be cottage gardener needs to be warned, however, that this look is deceptive. Creating, and even more so maintaining, a successful garden in the cottage style is hard work.

The informality of appearance belies the art and graft involved. But if you want to learn to love your plants and have the time, a cottage garden may be the garden for you.

Essentials

It doesn't matter if your house is not a cottage, but ideally the garden should be compact. The surroundings are important. Boundaries in particular need to be in keeping with the style of the garden. True cottagers were gardening gleaners and used what came to hand and so simplicity of materials is best. A wattle or hurdle fence for example is more in keeping than something complicated or metallic, and picket fencing, recycled pallets, or even chestnut paling can lend the right informal tone.

◀ *Filling your borders with traditional plants that suit your soil and situation is the ideal way to create the cottage garden look.*

stepping places between the apparently closely knit plants so that you can deadhead a rose, pick your currants, gooseberries or runner beans, adjust the supports and apply the hoe, as well as occasionally, in most summers, watering a thirsty phlox or spraying a mildewed michaelmas daisy.

In planning your own cottage garden, bear in mind that such gardens, while charming and colourful in spring and summer, can look dull in winter without evergreens to provide interest and colour. The essentially unstructured look, with winding paths and informal planting, also needs to include some structural elements if it's not to look confused and unplanned.

A good hedge also makes an attractive boundary for this style of garden. For higher hedges a natural look can be achieved using native plants such as hawthorn and blackthorn. Robust shrub roses such as the rugosa roses will make thick flowery hedges with red hips in the autumn and winter. Hornbeam or hazel make good deciduous hedges and hazel poles can be used as plant supports. Holly in the hedge makes the garden more interesting in winter, as do low dividing hedges of box, another evergreen. Lavender, rosemary or roses grown as a low to medium hedge defining areas within the garden will give flowers and scents as well as structure. Climbing plants such as honeysuckle or rambling roses can be used to add flowery confusion to a fence or hedge.

Maintenance

To maintain your cottage garden you will need to be adept with a hoe, for plants and weeds will seed themselves in the spaces. Don't be too ruthless in removing seedlings however, as some self-sown annuals will add their authentic cottage garden charm. It also pays to collect ripe seed from annuals and biennials such as poppies, pot marigolds and foxgloves so that you can sow them in your chosen places.

Planning and design

Many of the things you grow will need your attention during the summer, and it's as well to allow yourself a few

▶ *This ancient stone seat makes a perfect resting place in which to appreciate the scents, sights and sounds of a cottage garden.*

meadow gardens

Leave your garden to grow by itself and you'll get a tangle of ineradicable weeds, linked by scrambling bindweed and a blackberry thicket. It follows that growing a meadow hazily dotted with wild flowers like an Impressionist painting must be an art and the meadow as a garden must be deceptively contrived.

◄ *Grasses, swaying gently in the slightest summer breeze, are an essential ingredient of every successful meadow garden.*

Wild delights

What a dream of a garden the apparently artless meadow is – and many a plot has room for a little flowering meadow area of its own even when the rest is more conventionally cultivated. A tiny area of meadow in a lawn can be just as effective as a flower bed and can assuage that longing to be at one with nature. An important incidental feature of a wild meadow garden is that it attracts insects to the garden, bringing a peaceful summer hum. With luck, these will include beneficial insects that prey on garden pests, such as hoverflies, ladybirds and lacewings, and bees for pollination.

Many of the plants suitable for a meadow garden are wild native plants, but many more have been borrowed from gardens. Growing in grass and fending for themselves they will be smaller and more subtle. Growing a meadow garden is doing our bit for nature, as native flowers in the wild are a disappearing phenomenon, thanks to the use of herbicides, the ripping up of hedges, the grooming of the countryside and ever-spreading building, as well as the loss of wild areas in towns. But foxgloves, cornflowers, forget-me-nots, scabious, and verbascums were once as common in the wild as poppies on a building site and ox-eye daisies on a motorway bank, and these are typical meadow garden plants for us to grow from seed. Other plants for meadow planting, such as larkspur, tulips, love-in-a-mist and lupins, are wild flowers of another part of the world, and add a slightly foreign charm to the meadow.

Maintenance

The main work in presiding over a meadow garden is in the preparation and planting. After that the care needed is much less than that for a lawn or flower bed. Meadows are self-supporting once they are established and the plants must be allowed to seed themselves. This means that the flowers and grasses must

have gone to seed before you do any cutting.

Some cutting is necessary to keep down aggressively competitive weeds and grasses. So, depending on the look you want, cut in the autumn for a summer-flowering meadow or at the beginning of summer for spring meadows. The summer meadow can then be kept cut until late in the following spring to keep it at a reasonable height and to continue to discourage unwanted competitors, but it may be left if you prefer. A spring meadow can be mown or scythed during the summer unless it is also planted with summer flowers, in which case after an early summer cut it won't

▲ In this meadow carefully selected grasses and wild flowering plants mingle and flourish as nature would have chosen.

▶ Once established, a meadow garden will be self-supporting, but will look slightly different each year as different plants flourish.

need to be cut again until autumn.

Many people prefer to make the first cut a close one. In any case, the mowings must be raked up, not left on the soil to feed it, as the essence of a successful meadow garden is a soil of fairly low fertility. Every so often competing plants may gain the upper hand. Weeding your meadow will help to keep them under control, but sometimes the only answer is to start again.

scented gardens

Spring and summer are the best times for perfume in the garden, but winter offers its own heady delights – all the more so for being singled out through lack of competition. A scented garden has an added sensuous dimension, but some perfumes can be overpowering on a warm still day, so don't overdo it.

The role of scent

Scent is extremely evocative and appeals to a primitive and powerful part of the brain. The compelling power of scent to affect the emotions is intensified by the beauty of many scented plants. At the botanical level scent draws pollinators to a plant. Pale-coloured plants often give out their fragrance most strongly at night, when their paleness shows up best, and this is a two-pronged attraction for night pollinators, the moths. Colourful flowers attract day-time pollinators, the bees and butterflies, by their bright colour, and therefore in general the more brightly coloured flowers tend to offer less scent. Nature is generous, however, and gives us many colourful flowers (such as wall-flowers, some roses, and hyacinths) that are also strongly perfumed. Aromatic – as opposed to fragrant – plants have essential oils in their leaves to protect them from heat

◀ *Roses are among the most richly scented of all plants and no traditional garden would be complete without their distinctive presence.*

◄ *Combining a range of scented plants will produce a heady fragrance that hangs in the air and induces a romantic mood.*

many pleasures that you will want to linger and breathe in the different parts of the garden. They also seem to go best with a soft approach: curving lawns, which can act as a path unless the garden is large; loose planting, with plants allowed to merge into each other to blend the gentle colours of most scented plants. To coordinate the relaxed and natural theme, willow hurdles form a sympathetic material for plant supports and boundaries. And this is another garden theme that needs seating. A scented seat at the end of the garden will give you somewhere to rest when you're swooning from the mingled scents and pleasures of your plot.

exposure. The scents of the oils are intensified by heat and give out their best when grown in southern, Mediterranean-type climates. Less sensuous than invigorating, their scent indicates an antiseptic or medicinal value: thought to help protect the surrounding plants and flowers from disease.

Ingredients of the garden

Apart from the main distinction between fragrant and aromatic, it's very difficult to classify scents without referring to other scents – usually those of other flowers. So that roses are described as smelling of violets, lily of the valley, orange blossom, or even lemon, while pinks smell of cloves and choisya of orange blossom, although buddleia is agreed to smell of honey. Aromatherapists refer to the 'notes' of fragrance, descending from the light and evanescent top notes (for example, associated with lemony scents), to the heavy and lingering base notes, with middle (floral) notes in between. The base notes, found in plants such as the strongly scented lilies, jasmine, night-scented stocks, tobacco plants, and many roses, can be quite overpowering. It's a good idea to mix your plants so that a happy blend is inhaled on the air, with top, middle and base notes all participating. And it makes sense to measure out the more overpowering scents by having areas of quietly scented companions. Scented plants offer so

▶ *These beds of aromatic plants are surrounded by hedges of tightly clipped box, which has a curious scent of its own.*

rose gardens

Roses have been cultivated since ancient times and gardens to honour these lovely flowers have been devised wherever they will grow. Rose gardens can be a haven of scent, beauty and repose. But they do demand good planning and careful maintenance, because roses are not always easy to grow or manage.

◀ *In this rose garden a pathway featuring a series of timber arches provides the opportunities for climbing varieties.*

Design of a rose garden

The classic rose garden or rosarium was usually a garden within a garden. Geometrically designed, it was laid out within a square or oblong, and often quartered. Its regularly shaped beds were grouped symmetrically and separated by straight grass or gravel paths; at its centre a perfect circle or oval was set off by a bird bath, sun dial or piece of statuary. Wide arches covered with rambling roses might provide an entrance to the garden and frame its view, while within it other climbing roses would grow up central pillars or be trained along swags of heavy rope suspended between posts. The garden was usually defined by a formal hedge of box, yew, lavender or rosemary. Well–placed seating allowed enjoyment of the fragrance and beauty of the garden, as well as the structure of the design.

This might seem excessively formal for a smaller garden wholly made over to

▶ *In this classic rose garden, the beds have been edged with aromatic lavender – a traditional choice that complements the roses.*

roses, but there is still much to borrow from the classic rosarium. Treated informally, many of the ingredients can be copied to make a garden with a 'time stands still' feel to it. For instance, a sheltering evergreen hedge provides a perfect backdrop; box, rugosa roses or shrubby herbs make low to medium hedges giving structure and a textural continuity within the garden; instead of sturdy-looking pillars, hazel wigwams can be placed strategically to give inexpensive and natural-looking support to climbing roses and to add high points within the planting. Curving borders and informal planting in deep beds can help to give a relaxed feel to an otherwise formal gardening approach. Grass, brick, stone, timber, gravel – in fact all the traditional and natural materials – make good surfaces between borders.

Planning the garden

Roses like light, air, shelter and rich, deep soil, so for a start you need to be sure you have the right sort of plot. Plan carefully, bearing in mind the eventual size of the plants and whether or not they can be kept smaller by pruning, as well as the way each plant grows and its colour and scent. It's difficult to get a rose to grow where another one has been established, so after a few years it won't be possible to move the plants around.

Today there are many roses that flower either repeatedly or continuously right up till the autumn, so it's possible to choose roses that together will produce flowers over the longest possible season. Roses that have additional attractions, such as red hips or a pleasing

◀ *Roses provide a feast of sumptuous flowers – often deliciously scented – to be enjoyed throughout the warm summer months.*

shape, add an extra dimension and a happy choice of companion plants provides contrast.

Companion planting

The spires of plants such as foxgloves or delphiniums, campanula, and tall, graceful trumpet lilies look lovely growing among roses, while shade lovers such as violas, geraniums or heucheras can be used as underplanting. Clematis mingles blissfully with a climbing rose; burgeoning peonies or oriental poppies make a welcome contrast.

In open areas lavender, santolina and sage, or nepeta (catmint) will add an aromatic scent to the roses' sweetness. The idea is not to be too free with companions, but to use fairly bold groups here and there, while underplanting at the roses' feet can thread its way through the whole garden to unite the scheme.

flower arrangers' gardens

Even a small garden can produce a wealth of attractive flowers and foliage for cutting and displaying indoors. They are usually provided by herbaceous perennials and hardy and half-hardy annuals, although the leaves of many evergreen shrubs and climbers can also be added to arrangements.

Herbaceous perennials

These are ideal for providing flowers and leaves for summer arrangements, when they are fresh and bright. Most flowers and leaves are taken from plants growing in borders, but where space allows grow a few in a spare corner.

Never cut flowers from wilting plants because they soon fade. Water the plants the day before and cut them early in the morning. Place them in a bucket filled with water and in a cool room for 24 hours. Cut each stem at a 45-degree angle and remove the lower leaves.

Among the many herbaceous plants you can grow are *Achillea filipendulina* (fern-leaf yarrow), *Alstroemeria* (Peruvian lily), *Aster amellus*, *A. novae-angliae*, *A. novi-belgii*, *Catananche caerulea* (cupid's dart), *Coreopsis verticillata*, *Leucanthemum × maximum*, *Limonium latifolium*, *Lysimachia punctata* (yellow loosestrife), *Phlox paniculata*, *Rudbeckia laciniata*, *Solidago* (goldenrod) and *Tanacetum* (pyrethrum).

Hardy and half-hardy annuals

These enable flower-arranging enthusiasts to have a different range of fresh, bright-faced flowers each year and

▲ *A border packed with a medley of plants creates a reservoir of colourful flowers and differently shaped leaves for cutting.*

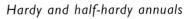

STAR PLANTS

Alchemilla mollis

Achillea filipendulina

Calendula officinalis

Coreopsis verticillata

Elaeagnus pungens 'Maculata'

Leucanthemum × maximum

Lysimachia punctata

Phlox paniculata

they are cut and prepared for display just like herbaceous perennials. They include *Calendula officinalis* (pot marigold), *Cosmos bipinnatus* (cosmea), *Delphinium consolida* (larkspur), *Gaillardia* (blanket flower), *Gypsophila elegans* (baby's breath), *Iberis umbellata* (globe candytuft), *Lathyrus odoratus* (sweet pea), *Nigella damascena* (love-in-a-mist), and *Reseda odorata* (mignonette).

Besides providing fresh flowers, a few hardy and half-hardy annuals can be grown to provide flowers for drying. They include *Celosia* (cockscomb), *helichrysum*, *Limonium sinuatum* and *Moluccella laevis* (bells of Ireland). Cut them with long stems, just as the flowers are opening. Tie them into small bunches and hang upside-down in a dry, well-ventilated room.

Attractive foliage

Many types of plants, including herbaceous perennials and evergreen shrubs and climbers, have foliage that can be added to flower arrangements. Those from herbaceous perennials include hostas with variegated and single-coloured leaves. The large, leathery, rounded leaves of bergenias are ideal as a background display. Those of *Alchemilla mollis* (lady's mantle) are daintier and their gentle lime-green colour is not so dramatic.

Evergreen shrubs such as *Elaeagnus pungens* 'Maculata' are dramatic, with shiny green leaves splashed gold, while those of *Elaeagnus × ebbingei* are leathery

and silver-grey. During early summer the stems of the *Lonicera nitida* 'Baggeson's Gold' (golden Chinese honeysuckle) look good, while the leaves of *Brachyglottis* 'Sunshine', better known as *Senecio* 'Sunshine', add a soft grey quality. Some displays benefit from stems of evergreen shrubs meandering at the edges. They include variegated vincas and small and large-leaved *Hedera* (ivy).

SEED HEADS FOR DRYING

Dried seed heads taken from herbaceous perennials create distinctive features, especially during winter. There are many plants to choose from, including:

Acanthus mollis (bear's breeches)

Dictamnus albus (burning bush)

Echinops ritro (globe thistle)

Iris foetidissima (stinking Iris)

Limonium platyphyllum (sea lavender)

Onopordum acanthium (scotch thistle)

Physalis alkekengi (Chinese lantern)

▲ *Sweet peas introduce a feast of colour to gardens, as well as providing flowers in many colours for decoration indoors.*

▲ *The stiffly erect flower heads of* Acanthus mollis *(bear's breeches) create dramatic features in gardens and flower displays.*

grass and bamboo gardens

Now extremely popular, grasses and bamboos can be used in all kinds of ways, from edging borders to creating screens. And some are ideal for adding to fresh flower arrangements and for drying for winter displays. There are both annual and perennial grasses, while bamboos are long-lived perennials.

▲ *The ornamental grass Miscanthus sinensis has a relaxed and arching nature; do not constrict it as its natural shape will be spoiled.*

Perennial grasses

Use these to fill entire beds on their own; there is a large range of heights, textures and colours. They can also be combined with annual types in ornamental grass borders.

Some perennial grasses are ideal for positioning along the edge of a border. They include *Festuca glauca*, about 23cm/9in high with blue-grey leaves,

BAMBOOS FOR CONTAINERS

A few bamboo varieties can be planted in large pots, tubs or wooden boxes, although eventually they will need to be planted in the garden or taken out and divided; this is best done in early summer. Because the roots of bamboos in containers can easily be damaged in cold winters, choose only the hardiest types such as:

Fargesia murieliae (umbrella bamboo) – 1.8–2.4m/6–8ft high.

Pleioblastus auricomus (golden-haired bamboo) – 90cm–1.2m/3–4ft high.

Pseudosasa japonica (arrow bamboo) – 2.4–3.6m/8–12ft high.

and the more dramatic *Melica altissima* 'Atropurpurea', growing about 1.5m/5ft high with deep mauve spikelets that sweep downwards. It is ideal for use fresh or dried in flower arrangements. *Stipa tenuissima* 'Angel Hair' rises to about 75cm/2½ft and bears soft, wispy pony-tails. *Miscanthus sacchariflorus* (amur silver grass) is probably the most dramatic of all perennial grasses. Rapidly growing each year to about 3m/10ft high, it is ideal for forming a screen. Space the plants about 45cm/18in apart; the first year, when becoming established, they may rise to only 1.8m/6ft, but the following season grow much higher. Others include *Miscanthus sinensis purpurascens* with purple-tinged stems reaching a height of 1.5m/5ft.

Annual grasses

Ideal for creating different displays each year, these can be sown where they are to flower and are useful for filling gaps in herbaceous and mixed borders. Many can be cut and dried for use in winter decorations. They include the well-known *Briza maxima* (quaking grass) with graceful, pendent, nodding flowers, *Hordeum jubatum* (squirrel grass), and *Lagurus ovatus* (hare's-tail grass), which develops soft, fur-like, silky flowerheads.

Bamboos for all gardens

Invariably hardy plants, these are actually woody grasses and have a wide range of foliage and stems to add colour and interest. Most are evergreen, a few are semi-evergreen in cold winters and some are deciduous. They add the sound of gentle rustling and are also good for cloaking unsightly features. A few bamboos, such as *Pleioblastus auricomus* (golden-haired bamboo), are about 1.5m (5ft) high and can be grown in a 25cm/10in-wide pot on a patio, while others rapidly rise to 3m/10ft or more.

Three of the most popular bamboos are *Fargesia murieliae* with graceful, arching, bright green canes, *Fargesia nitida* with purple stems and narrow, bright-green leaves, and *Pseudosasa japonica* with lance-shaped, dark-green leaves. Some are more distinctive, such as the square-stemmed *Chimonobambusa quadrangularis* and black-stemmed *Phyllostachys nigra*.

▲ *Where slugs and snails are a problem, create a shingle or gravel area and stand pots of ornamental grasses and bamboos on it.*

◄ *Pleioblastus auricomus (golden-haired bamboo) is a dwarf variety with golden variegated leaves, ideal for borders or containers.*

seaside gardens

If you garden right by the sea you can't ignore it. Coastal winds can waft sea salt several miles inland, so even away from the sound of the wave you can be prey to seaside conditions. Coastal gardens offer a challenge and the first problem you need to address is usually that of providing shelter.

Seaside designs

A garden within sight of the sea is crying out for the full seaside treatment, complete with nautical ingredients and finds from the shore: driftwood, sand, gravel and pebbles, shells, anchor chains and even nets or ropes will all be at home here.

A smooth green lawn would be almost impossible to maintain, and would look ill at ease in this setting, whereas hard surfaces are much more appropriate. Likewise the soil will be inhospitable to most plants, and you will need to concentrate on maritime species, and on creating a design through objects and materials as well as plants – although of course you can use containers and bought compost for those plants that demand more fertile soil.

Solid timber works well as a material of many uses in a real seaside garden, evocative of old boats and quay-sides, but it's best not to use tarred wood in proximity to plants as tarry poisons continue to seep out for many years – to the plants' distress. If you want to lighten new timber to give it a bleached salt-sea look, the best treatment is to paint it with an opaque white wood stain that is safe for animals and plants.

Dealing with exposure

One of the things a coastal situation has in common with rooftops is exposure to the wind, and here the winds will be a nuisance not only because of their buffeting, but also because they carry salt with them from the sea. Luckily there are several salt-wind-resistant shrubs and trees that can be used to help to break the force of the wind, planted singly or grouped in key places. A strong screen in

◀ *Decking works perfectly in a seaside garden, especially if the timbers are treated for that salted, worn-away look.*

◀ *In a coastal garden, make sure you choose tough plants that can put up with sea spray, strong winds and heavy rain.*

and works well if you want to hide an unpleasant view. Panels for fences and trellis screens are also, of course, readily available, and a great deal cheaper than the materials for walls, as well as being much easier to put together yourself.

As an alternative to a built boundary or enclosure a seaside hedge will filter the wind and give shade and shelter while being good to look at in its own right. While the hedge is getting established a temporary netting windbreak can be set up, stretched between posts on the windward side to give protection. Juniper, broom, wormwood, Spanish broom and fuschia are resistant, shrubby plants, ideal for growing in coastal areas.

the form of a fence or wall that is perforated to let through light and reduce the wind's strength without creating turbulence is sometimes preferable, especially to give privacy in a small area. A fence need not have a straight top and can be painted to enhance the garden scheme rather than left as it is. In the bright coastal light bold colours work well, as does matt white, while pale ones can look insipid, unless placed in an area of shade, where they look cool.

For total privacy a stone or brick wall will provide complete shelter but a solid barrier does cause wind turbulence.

Furthermore, a solid wall has the disadvantage that you can't get a glimpse of the view through it if there's a good one. Despite these disadvantages, if you live in an area where stone is the natural local material, a low stone wall, traditionally built, can be very attractive, particularly where you are creating a courtyard-style garden immediately next to the house. Generally, however, a pierced wall or fence, or heavy-duty trellis is more effective as a windbreak,

▶ *Natural objects bring a seaside garden to life; this old rowing boat looks as though the sea has carried it straight into the garden.*

Mediterranean gardens

Endless blue skies, warm breezes and little rain epitomize Mediterranean gardens, especially to visitors who know them only through summer visits. However, they do vary dramatically throughout the year and, although the summers are hot and dry, there is often a radical change in winter.

◄ *Bright surfaces, coloured tiles and plants with variegated, dagger-like leaves, such as* Agave americana *'Marginata', create a vibrant setting.*

Mediterranean plants

Spring-flowering bulbs and tuberous-rooted plants soon burst into flower as the cool of winter is replaced by spring warmth, while annuals burgeon into growth ready for later flowering. Native plants include rosemary, myrtle, *Cistus* (rock rose), laurel, olives, figs and dwarf palms. Best known is *Cupressus sempervirens* (Italian or Mediterranean cypress), particularly the narrow forms. They epitomize Mediterranean gardens and are frequently seen in small clusters.

Silver-leaved plants are better able to survive hot, dry conditions than plants with green leaves. They include shrubby and herbaceous *Artemisias*. Plants with hairy leaves are also equipped for hot regions. For example, *Stachys byzantina* (lamb's tongue), has oval leaves densely covered with white, silvery hairs. *Cistus* (rock rose) has leaves that emit resinous scents and it also thrives in warm areas.

Warm terraces

Wide terraces with ornate stone balustrades are ideal areas for enjoying outdoor life. These areas are also perfect for plants in a wide range of containers. Where possible, position them in partial shade, which helps prevent the compost becoming too hot, and reduces the amount and frequency of watering.

Shade is as important for people as for plants, and a tall tree with a climber such as *Clematis montana* (Mountain clematis) clambering through its branches creates a spectacular feature when flowering in late spring and early summer. Additionally, it provides summer shade and is splendid for creating a cool outdoor living area. If it becomes too large, cut it back as soon as the flowers fade. Other climbers create shade, and where there is a large pergola, a wisteria can be planted to clamber over it, although it needs more pruning than the clematis, and it will not create such a dense canopy of shade.

Brightening steps

Wide flights of steps that link terraces with lower levels need not be solely functional. Position clusters of plants in containers at the top and bottom, especially if the lower area is wider. Narrow steps, perhaps positioned to one side of a terrace and connecting to a lower garden, can have their sides clothed in trailing plants. If the sides have a dry stone wall, plant the yellow-flowered *Aurinia saxatilis* (still better known as *Alyssum saxatile*) and the contrasting *Aubrieta deltoidea* (aubretia) for a wealth of purple to rose-lilac flowers during late spring and early summer.

TEMPERATE PALM

A few palms are sufficiently hardy to survive temperate areas and they include the Chinese *Trachycarpus fortunei*. Plant it in well-drained but moisture-retentive soil in a warm, sunny, sheltered position. Placed near a terrace it will provide shade. It takes about 15 years to grow to 3m/10ft high and has large, pleated leaves up to 90cm/3ft wide and the bonus of a trunk covered in wiry black fibre.

▲ Even the smallest paved area can be given a Mediterranean nature. Colour washed walls and metal-framed furniture complete the design.

◄ Colourful pots with low-growing and slightly bushy plants are ideal for positioning along the edges of steps. Ensure that they are secure.

Japanese gardens

Japanese gardens exude serenity, peace and contemplation. They have a simple, uncluttered, well-defined nature that creates tranquillity and contentment. The design of early Japanese gardens was influenced in the seventh century by the return of a Japanese ambassador from China.

Gravel gardening

Few features in Japanese gardens are as restful to the eye as a gravel garden, perhaps formed of a large, level area of gravel and well-spaced groupings of two, three or five large rocks that assume the nature of small islands. The gravel is raked to create the impression of shallow waves. Large areas of gravel can be given extra interest by laying a stepping stone path across them, but avoid splitting up the area and producing two seas of gravel. If laying a further path use smaller stone to create a less dominant feature.

Paths and rivers

In slightly less formal areas – and where there is a gentle slope – use pebbles instead of gravel and create two or three paths and rivers. Using large, irregular-shaped stepping stones and surrounding them with coloured shale will create the impression of a stream. Where the area is moderately steep, form a narrow stream, using stones and shale but in flatter areas make it wider. This will give a more natural, harmonious outline.

Water and bridges

Moving water is an essential element in some Japanese gardens. Tumbling and splashing water can be achieved with a small pump and this creates an exciting feature throughout the year. Japanese wooden bridges are distinctive and often have a misleading appearance of frailty. Additionally, where just a simple bridge

◀ *Japanese gardens have a serenity unmatched by any other style of gardening. Large rocks, gravel and bamboos are the main features of many of these gardens.*

is needed over a narrow stream, thick planks of wood or long slabs of stone are attractive and easy to use. Where the stream is wide and the current is slow, several pieces of stone or wood can be linked. Large stepping stones also look good and, occasionally, are positioned down the centre of a stream.

TEA GARDENS

Tea gardens play an essential role in the tea ceremony. In a tranquil setting, those taking part first assemble in the garden to cast off worldly cares before drinking tea. Gravel and stepping stones are prime features, as are trees, shrubs and ferns that have a timeless and contemplative nature. Ephemeral flowers, however, do not feature because they reveal the changing seasons and the passing of time.

Shrubs and bamboos

Bamboos epitomize Japanese gardens and many grow well beside streams. Some varieties can also be easily grown in a large tub or a square, wooden container; suitable bamboos are described in more detail on pages 22–23.

Two small trees that characterize Japanese gardens, and which are ideal in tubs, are the Japanese maples, *Acer palmatum dissectum* and *Acer p.d. atropurpurea*, the former with deeply cut green leaves and the latter with bronze-red foliage. They are both deciduous and have a wide, dome-like outline. The evergreen *Fatsia japonica* can also be planted in a large container. Its large, rich glossy green leaves with seven to nine lobes provide a good structural contrast.

▲ *Small trees with finely divided green or bronze-purple leaves are instantly associated with Japanese gardens.*

▼ *Meandering streams, simple bridges and gravel paths bordered with low-growing plants create a restful ambience.*

Zen gardens

A Japanese Zen garden is understood not in terms of its ingredients but only by looking at its overall meaning – nothing is fortuitous or haphazard. All the elements employed in the garden have a symbolic significance related to a quest for spiritual enlightenment. Restraint and simplicity are the keys.

What are the elements?

Whether or not we understand Zen symbolism, we can borrow ideas from Japanese gardens to make our own peaceful and beautiful retreats that, with care, do not look too much out of place in a Western setting. When you have a cuppa at the end of the garden, perhaps you will think about your spiritual journey through the world. If not, it will still be a nice calm and peaceful place to sit.

While some elements come from Buddhist monastery gardens, the Zen garden of today is largely based on a Japanese invention of early medieval times, and its development responded to the practices of the tea ceremony, which was given mystical and ritual dimensions by the Zen priests and their disciples who took part in it. The participants at a tea ceremony reflected on nature and sought inner stillness by contemplating flowers, pottery and beautifully illustrated calligraphic scrolls in the confines of a tea house. The Zen garden was the medium through which they passed on their way to the sanctum of contemplation.

A spiritual journey

The garden sought to imitate nature in the wild, and provided a path representing a mountain journey – a metaphor for the spiritual journey in search of the eternal. So the essence of the Zen garden is that we move through

◄ *Traditionally the clean, simple design of a Zen garden creates a retreat, and the possibility for quiet, tranquil contemplation.*

▶ *Boulders and gravel in Zen gardens symbolize mountains and water, associated in Buddhist thought with visions of paradise.*

it and lose our baser selves on the way. The ingredients, charged with symbolism, were an entrance (the journey's beginning), a path (the way to knowledge or enlightenment), a seat on which to break the journey and pause in meditation, a gate or threshold, beyond which to move on, leaving behind the social world of the city and entering the world of nature. Finally, there was somewhere to wash the hands, representing a mountain stream and symbolic of purification, and at the journey's end, a tea house as a place of final contemplation.

Symbolism in the garden

Paradise in Buddhist thought was symbolized by mountains surrounded by water, and in a Zen garden water and rocks represent these elements. Much play is made of the contrast between rocks or pebbles and water. When using boulders it's important to lay the stone in accordance with its natural grain. (If you are serious about it, you won't even lay the stone on its side while manoeuvring it into position.) Placing the stone in this way makes sense aesthetically, and is

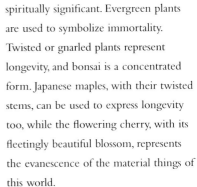

spiritually significant. Evergreen plants are used to symbolize immortality. Twisted or gnarled plants represent longevity, and bonsai is a concentrated form. Japanese maples, with their twisted stems, can be used to express longevity too, while the flowering cherry, with its fleetingly beautiful blossom, represents the evanescence of the material things of this world.

Water itself need not be present. The raked gravel of Buddhist gardens, which has now caught on in the West, is used to represent flowing water. Raking it quietly each morning or evening can be a soothing meditation. Rocks or boulders set within the gravel represent the water-surrounded mountains of paradise. They should be placed at the far end of the garden, as paradise is always distant. Straight lines are to be avoided – the spirit of contemplation follows best a winding path – but they can be broken, and begun again, and this will slow down the rush of energy that is not conducive to contemplation. Overall balance in design is achieved by a measured lack of symmetry.

Colours chosen for a Zen garden should be subtle and limited. The natural colours of stone, timber and bamboo, and the green of bamboo plants and evergreen shrubs help form a calm, quiet backdrop.

◀ *This contemporary interpretation of Zen principles features neatly raked gravel and a delicate purple iris planted in bamboo.*

31

container and
patio gardening

Whatever the size and shape of a garden there is always space for a patio or terrace on which to grow plants in containers. These range from hanging baskets to window boxes, troughs, tubs and urns. Roof gardens are another possibility, but ensure that the roof's structure is sound. Stone sinks on a patio enable small bulbs and miniature conifers to be grown in an alpine setting, while raised beds allow disabled gardeners to pursue their hobby.

patio gardens

A patio is not necessarily an enclosed garden, but is best if sheltered for privacy and protected from draughts. There is no reason for a patio to be at the back of the house. If the front garden is warm and sunny, and you enjoy some privacy from the neighbours, why not make that your outdoor room?

Outdoor living

Ideally the patio garden will be right next to the house, preferably situated so that you can spill out on to it and use it as an extension to a living room or dining room. Because you want to use it for sunbathing and for outdoor eating it will have a great deal in common with a sunny seaside garden and with sheltered courtyard gardens. You don't have to devote your whole garden to a patio, but if the plot is small this may well be an ideal design solution.

A patio garden is perfect for people who are too busy to spend a great deal of time on the garden and who want to use it mainly as living space. The area should have a firm surface, and at least part of this should be suitable for furniture. A pebbled patio is not usually very successful as chairs and tables can't stand on it properly. The best choices are paving, brickwork or timber decking, which makes a pleasant surface for sunbathing and is less unforgiving when plates and glasses are dropped on it. Whatever you choose, the surface is going to be a major investment in this type of garden, and it's wise to consider carefully which is best for you. In a large area you might like to vary the materials used, and provide planting space between stone slabs or bricks, or in gravel to avoid too hard a look.

◀ *Carefully selected, well-placed plants will soften the overall effect of a patio which could easily be dominated by hard landscaping materials.*

◀ *Established planting and the use of trellises provide shelter from wind and prying eyes.*

Equipping your patio

Enjoy planning your barbecue equipment and patio furniture. In the long run it is generally best to make a serious investment and get well-designed tables and chairs that look good and will last well. If you buy hardwood, cast-iron or good-quality aluminium furniture you can leave it out in all weathers. Wood will need oiling every year and metal furniture may need painting occasionally, but both will enhance your garden and age well. If you buy plastic you will need somewhere to store it during the winter – and it doesn't have the same style. Resin café tables and chairs are a possible alternative and pack away neatly for winter storage.

Cooking outdoors

If you expect to be having frequent meals outdoors, consider building a barbecue into a wall on the patio as part of the design. This may be a job for a qualified builder. However, a free-

standing barbecue, in materials that blend with walls or floor surfaces, is within a confident home improver's scope. The essential ingredients are a back and two sides, with a burning rack raised above

ground level so that air can feed the fire, and a cooking rack above it. The rack should be about 90cm/3ft high for comfort, and should be wide enough to have areas at each side that are not directly above the fire, so that cooked food can be pushed to the side to keep warm. The side walls should be wide enough to hold utensils, food supplies and perhaps plates. A shallow pit below the burning area will help to prevent ashes blowing about the patio. However, a fixed barbecue may be rather unsightly in winter.

Whatever the design of your barbecue, it should not be placed beneath overhanging trees, or close to shrubs or flowers, which might catch fire. Ideally it will be close to the kitchen so that supplies can be kept refrigerated until they are needed and easily conveyed to the cooking area.

Lighting will enhance the patio and plants at night time. And, without spoiling the atmosphere, it's a good idea to make sure that the area around the barbecue and the path to and from the kitchen are well lit for safety. These safety lights can always be turned off once you are seated for romantic dining by candlelight or lamplight.

◀ *A patio can provide privacy or a romantic retreat. This tucked away corner is an example of a covered patio space.*

courtyard gardens

A courtyard garden can be made from a space which is partially or totally enclosed. It's usually near the house, perhaps linked to it by a patio or terrace, and bounded by walls, fences or hedges. While some are suntraps, a courtyard at basement level is often cool and shady – a place for different shades of green.

◄ *Black bamboo in galvanized metal containers contributes much to this minimalist courtyard. Stylish dining furniture completes the look.*

An outdoor room

A small enclosed garden at the back of a terraced town house is the ideal candidate for the courtyard treatment. Well-defined by boundaries, it offers a private area generally with no view to worry about losing. Mellow country cottages often have a paved, cobbled or brick-set area immediately outside the house, with or without a garden beyond, and these areas too make perfect courtyard gardens, although here it may be important not to become too enclosed, if this would risk losing views of the rest of the garden or of the countryside beyond.

Being (generally) next to the house a courtyard becomes another room – a perfect place for dining and entertaining, sun-bathing, dozing, or even to sit and work in. Apart from its 'room' quality, the essence of the courtyard is also its hard-landscaping. If you have the stone or

▶ *In a suntrap courtyard a spiky-leaved plant grown in a classic terracotta container will give a Mediterranean touch.*

brick floor already, be advised to keep it. If not, choose materials that will suit those of your house. Small-sized units are best, except in a large area.

Again your courtyard may have natural boundaries already. If not you will need to start by supplying boundaries for enclosure. Be aware that the higher they go the greater your privacy but also the greater the shade. Walls in the same material as the house are unbeatable, with wires or trellis attached firmly to give support to climbing plants. A dense evergreen hedge will offer great privacy but will take several years to grow and will rob the limited amount of soil of its nutrients. Both hedges and walls create dry areas at the base which are inhospitable to plants. Lightweight fencing can be a very satisfactory alternative, acting as a screen and support for plants, while still letting in light. Screening trellis is right in formal settings while hazel or willow hurdles look good in a more rural country garden.

Structuring the garden

Restraint and some formality are required for courtyard gardens. Decide on your theme and don't try to cram too many ideas into a small space. A lot of the planting will probably be in containers, but it's worth contemplating building raised planting areas filled with earth (with drainage) as these can add structure and will also need less watering than containers. Again, the materials used should be in sympathy with those of the house and with the enclosure. You may well be looking at the garden from above a lot of the time, for example from a first-floor living room or bedroom, so make sure that the scheme will look as well from this angle as it does when you are actually sitting in it. Because of the shelter it gains from its boundaries a courtyard can be warm and still at night, and is a natural place for fitting subtle lighting for enjoying the evening. Good-quality garden furniture can be a key garden feature.

◀ *Courtyard gardens can be home to many plants, both growing in containers and trained on trellis against the wall.*

roof gardens

Some of the most exciting modern gardens are those designed for roofs, where with fewer precedents as a starting point, the imagination can take off. And with many problems to face, your ingenuity is called into play to find a multitude of brilliant solutions in terms of plants and overall design.

Problems to be solved

The problems associated with roof gardens are manifold: safety, the challenge to the strength and water-resistance of the roof, and the exposed position being at the top of the list. Before you start there is the question of whether the roof can take the strain and bear the weight of a garden. This is something that must be resolved by a qualified surveyor. Roofs tend to be exposed to the wind, and often also to others' view if there are higher buildings around. Unless you are lucky enough to have a decent parapet to which you can fix a windbreak you will have to take advice about this matter too. Then there is the question of access, which makes bringing plants and materials to the site quite a challenge. The materials used on the roof will almost certainly have to be lightweight and easily portable, partly in order to convey them there and partly because there will probably be weight restrictions

◀ *A roof-top garden can be as innovative as you like, as this modernistic design shows.*

in force. When laying a surface you will have to make sure that rainwater can still run off the roof and drain away as before, and that it will not get trapped and cause damage (for example, it is not a good idea to fix decking bearers crosswise against the 'fall' or incline of the roof where they will impede the run-off of rainwater).

Lightweight solutions

Light asbestos slabs (perfectly safe), lightweight decking in pressure-treated timber, gravel or stone chippings are all possible materials for the roof surface in preference to heavy stone or concrete paving. Screening for privacy, enclosure and shelter should be strongly constructed and heavy-duty to withstand the buffeting of the wind and must be securely fixed and bolted to the walls to ensure your safety. A built-in store for tools and barbecue equipment will be

▶ *Balconies have comparable problems, and solutions, to roofs on a smaller scale.*

welcome to save hauling things in and out. A convenient water supply will be necessary as planting compost will dry out quickly in this situation – it may be possible to install a rainwater tank on the roof, against a wall to take the weight, but automatic or semi-automatic irrigation will be necessary.

Plant containers can be fibreglass, plastic or aluminium, as well as timber, and if necessary they can be bracketed to the perimeter wall so that their weight isn't transferred to the roof surface. Because of weight limits lightweight compost will be needed for planting.

Enjoying your position

If, as often in older houses, the roof is at first-floor level over a back extension, with the house wall behind it, a patio

can be created by building a timber frame bolted to the wall. Plants can be grown over this to make a green and shady sitting area.

Basking on a roof can make you feel rather smug – a bit like being on horseback and talking down to people on foot. Getting a bird's eye view of the neighbourhood is bound to make you feel one-up. So when possible enjoy this by maintaining a sense of height and keeping the view, if only in part, by using strong, open trellis. And if you place plant containers along the top of a parapet wall they must be securely fixed to the parapet and carefully watered to make sure there is no danger of their falling off and injuring, or dripping onto, anyone below.

◀ *Screened for privacy and shelter, this roof makes good use of lightweight timber for decking and fitted seating.*

window box colour

By using a combination of spring, summer and winter displays it is possible to have a colourful garden throughout the year. Spring displays are mainly formed of bulbs and biennials, while summer arrangements rely on bedding plants. Winter displays usually depend on foliage plants.

Creating a year-round display

In addition to an attractive window box – positioned either on a window-ledge, or on brackets attached to the wall and about 20cm/8in below the ledge (if a casement type) – three inner boxes are needed. By planting these with seasonal displays, the window can be given a fresh feature three times a year.

▲ *Decorative, plaque-like plant containers create distinctive features when mounted on a wall. Eventually they become drenched in colour.*

✸ Spring displays – plant these in the autumn using spring-flowering bulbs such as hyacinths, tulips and *Narcissus* (daffodils), and biennials like *Erysimum* (wallflowers), *Myosotis* (Forget-me-not) and double daisies. When planted, put the container in a cool, well-drained sheltered part of the garden. In spring, when the bulbs are breaking into bud and the biennials are starting to flower, remove the winter display and replace with the spring arrangement.

✸ Summer displays – plant in late spring and initially place in a sheltered, frost-free position outdoors or in a well-ventilated conservatory. In early summer, when the spring display is nearly over, replace with this one.

✸ Winter displays – in autumn, as soon as the summer display has been dulled by frost, remove it and put in the winter arrangement. This is mainly formed of hardy foliage plants, such as small pots of *Aucuba japonica* 'Variegata', small-leaved *Hedera* (ivy), miniature and slow growing conifers, winter-flowering *Erica* (heath), *Calluna* (heather), variegated forms of

Euonymus japonicus and *Hebe* × *andersoniana* 'Variegata'.

Wall baskets and mangers

These resemble hanging baskets cut in half and secured to a wall, but they are larger and able to hold more compost. They look good in any position and are especially useful for securing to walls abutting pavements or alongside mews cottages. Wall basket and manger displays are more limited than window boxes and can have only spring and summer arrangements. Spring displays are planted directly into the container in autumn and left until they flower in spring. When over, all the plants are removed, fresh compost put in its place and a summer display planted. This lasts until autumn, when the spring display is planted.

STAR PLANTS

Aucuba japonica 'Variegata'

Lobularia maritima

Muscari armeniacum

Three seasonal medleys

The range of possible plants is wide but the following suggestions are a fail-safe, attractive design for each season.

❀ Spring – this can be a combination of plants, using biennials such as *Erysimum* (wallflower), double daisies and *Myosotis* (forget-me-not), and bulbs like *Muscari armeniacum* (grape hyacinth), *Tulipa greigii* and *T. fosteriana*.

❀ Summer – for a colourful display plant a combination of trailing lobelia, zonal pelargoniums, *Lobularia maritima* (sweet alyssum), tuberous-rooted begonias and summer-flowering *Viola* (pansy). Position trailing plants at one end or along the front, with the begonias in the centre. Container-grown plants will need some feeding and regular watering throughout any dry weather.

❀ Winter – this can be a grouping of foliage plants such as small-leaved *Hedera helix* 'Glacier' (ivy), variegated *Euonymus japonicus* and the dwarf conifer *Chamaecyparis lawsoniana* 'Pygmaea Argentea'. The winter-flowering *Erica* (heath) adds colour.

▶ *Use upright and bushy plants to create a display at the top of a window box, and trailing foliage types to drape the front in colour.*

▼ *Instead of planting summer-flowering plants directly into compost in a window box, they can be left in their pots and replaced as they fade.*

HERBS IN WINDOW BOXES

A window box outside a kitchen window creates the opportunity to have a wide range of readily available herbs. Choose a medley of low-growing plants, such as mint, thyme, chives, parsley, marjoram and French tarragon. The range of mints is wide and includes spearmint and applemint. Leave individual plants in their pots and place them on a layer of shingle in the window box, so that their rims are slightly below the top. Pack moist peat around the pots to keep the compost moist and cool.

hanging baskets

To many gardeners, hanging baskets are the epitome of summer colour. They enliven walls with bright flowers and foliage, and are ideal for brightening small gardens. Indeed, they invariably look extremely good in courtyards and small paved areas, and in entrances and porches.

Displaying hanging baskets

These can be displayed in many ways, perhaps one either side of a window and about 38cm/15in from the frame, creating a special feature. You could also enliven the edges of verandahs by positioning hanging baskets along them.

◀ *Brick columns are a useful site for fixing a hanging basket from a bracket. Position the basket where it cannot be knocked.*

They introduce round and cascading features to an area invariably dominated by vertical and horizontal lines.

Where a wall is bland, position hanging baskets along it, but not near corners or where they might be knocked. To prevent people from knocking them, put tubs on the ground but not underneath the baskets because water will drip onto them. Brighten up carports in the same way as verandahs, again avoiding head-hitting positions. If you choose white or light-coloured plants the baskets will still be noticeable in the evening gloom. When using hanging baskets in lobbies and porches, make sure that drip-trays are built into them to prevent water spilling onto the floor below.

Choosing the plants

Choosing the right plants for hanging baskets is part of their success. Here are clues to eye-catching displays. Do not cram in too many plants; once established, fewer but bigger and healthier plants look better than a mass of plants, each fighting for survival. Additionally, do not use too many different types of plants. Mixed displays look good, but a dozen different plants will not look as attractive as only four or five types.

Also, when planting a mixed basket, choose a medley of trailing, bushy and upright plants. Select a showy plant for the centre, such as a fuchsia or upright geranium, with trailers around the edge and coming out of the basket's sides. When plants are bought from a nursery or garden centre, the choice of varieties may be limited. If you can grow your own, choose varieties that are compact or recommended for hanging baskets. As well as summer-flowering plants, use hardy perennials such as variegated small-leaved *Hedera* (ivy) and forms of *Glechoma hederacea* (ground ivy) with attractive foliage. Finally, unless you are able to spray plants regularly with insecticides, avoid those that are particularly prone to pests, such as nasturtiums, which attract blackflies.

Strawberries and tomatoes

Both create features that draw attention, but choose varieties with care. The strawberry 'Mignonette' is an alpine with small fruits that in France are used for decorating pastries. 'Temptation' is another suitable variety, with aromatic sweet fruits from mid-summer to the frosts of autumn. The bushy tomato 'Tumbler' is ideal for planting in hanging baskets, and produces small, sweet fruits.

▶ *To create a spectacular hanging basket, use a combination of upright, cascading and trailing plants. Additionally, daily watering is vital.*

SINGLE-SUBJECT HANGING BASKETS

The following produce eyecatching displays:

Calceolaria integrifolia 'Sunshine' – creates a dominant display packed with yellow, pouch-like flowers.

Fuchsias – use bushy and trailing types. Plants are sometimes slow to create a display, so ensure that they are well developed.

Impatiens (busy Lizzie) – bright colours.

Laurentia axillaris 'Stargazer' – a mass of five-petalled, 2.5cm/1in-wide flowers in a range of colours including blue, white and pink.

Lobelia (in mixed colours) – trailing varieties create a dazzling display.

Petunia grandiflora 'Double Cascade Burgundy Plum Vein' – cascading plant with giant, fully double, burgundy or plum-coloured flowers over the summer.

pots and tubs

These popular, versatile containers can accommodate plants of many sizes and types. The agapanthus, with tall stems bearing umbrella-like flowerheads, looks good in square, Versailles-type planters, while rounded, evergreen shrubs look better in large, round tubs.

Displaying pots and tubs

There are plants for all containers and places, and all you have to do is select the right combination. Small courtyards need at least one dominant plant and container around which other plants can be grouped, and for this position *Fatsia japonica* (false castor oil plant) is superb. Placed in a very large clay pot it needs a sheltered position in sun or shade. It is an evergreen shrub, ideal in towns and suited to container gardening.

The top of a flight of steps always looks better with several pots. In formal areas just one plant on each side looks distinctive, while for informal settings a group of small plants creates a more restful feature. On patios, a large trough under a window with distinctive pots and plants on each side creates a fine focal point.

In a rural setting, make home-made containers formed of three or four car tyres stacked and wired together, with a large, plastic bucket wedged in the top and planted with spring flowers such as polyanthus. Paint the tyres white for greater harmony with the polyanthus. In formal settings, especially in towns, position a small tub either side of an entrance and plant a clipped, half-standard *Laurus nobilis* (bay) in each. Ornate urns on high pedestals also create focal points and look good at junctions of wide gravel paths. Troughs, widely

◀ *Position pots alongside paths as well as on patios. Slightly burying pots keeps the compost cool and reduces the need to water them.*

available in materials from plastic to glass-fibre and reconstituted stone, can be positioned on the tops of bland walls or along patio edges, verandahs and balconies. Where there is just vertical space, choose plants like daffodils, but if cascading is a possibility, summer-flowering trailing plants can be used.

Foliage plants for tubs and pots

Foliage plants create permanency on patios and terraces and help to unify groups of plants, especially when partly formed of annuals. Their range is wide and evergreen shrubs with variegated leaves include *Aucuba japonica* 'Variegata' with green leaves splashed yellow, *Hebe × franciscana* 'Variegata' with glossy green leaves edged cream, *Hebe × andersonii* 'Variegata' with cream-variegated leaves, *Choisya ternata* 'Sundance' with golden leaves, and *Yucca filamentosa* 'Variegata' with its sword-like leaves edged and striped creamy yellow.

▶ *Brighten walls by attaching brackets that support pots of many sizes. These can be used in combination with hanging baskets.*

▼ *Clinical displays, formed of square containers planted with narrow-leaved, spiky plants, are ideal for a modern setting.*

CLIMBERS IN CONTAINERS

Several climbers can be grown in containers, but regular attention is needed to ensure that the compost does not become dry. Some are perennials, others are annuals raised from seed each year.

Clematis, large-flowered types – choose a tub or large pot. Flowers from early to late summer, depending on the variety, with a range of colours. Ornate metal railings look attractive when covered by the flowers.

Clematis macropetala – choose a large terracotta or wooden tub, fill its base with clean rubble, then well-drained compost. Put several plants with light and dark blue flowers around the top to encourage cascading.

Humulus lupulus 'Aureus' (yellow-leaved hop) – select a large tub for this herbaceous climber and form a wigwam of 1.5–1.8m/5–6ft-long canes. They become smothered in yellow leaves.

Ipomoea purpurea (morning glory) – grown as a half-hardy annual, with large, bell-like flowers in several colours.

Tropaeolum majus (nasturtium) – grown as a half-hardy annual, with flowers in several colours throughout summer.

stone sinks on patios

Where there is no space for a rock garden or even a scree bed, a stone sink on a patio or terrace is an ideal home for small rock garden plants, dwarf bulbs and miniature conifers. By selecting the right combination of plants you can have an attractive feature throughout the year.

▲ *Stone sinks are ideal for creating miniature gardens on patios. Positioning a sink on bricks helps to reduce the ravages of snails and slugs.*

Selecting and preparing a sink

Ideally, an old stone sink is best. However, a deep, white-glazed sink can easily be modified to give an attractive, well-worn appearance. This is done by scratching the surface, coating it with PVA and covering with a slightly moist mixture of equal parts of cement powder, sharp sand and peat.

Place the sink on four strong bricks; preferably, it should have a slight slope towards the drainage hole. Place a piece of perforated zinc over the drainage hole so it cannot get blocked, then a layer of broken clay pots or pebbles over the entire base to facilitate drainage. Spread a

POSITIONING A SINK GARDEN

Sink gardens need full sun or partial shade, and a position where they cannot be tripped over. Therefore, unless the patio or terrace is large with a rarely used corner, position a couple of columnar conifers in pots close to the sink to really mark it out. Light-coloured conifers are better than dark green ones, because they can be easily seen in the twilight.

2.5cm/1in-thick layer of sharp sand and half-fill with a mixture of equal parts of potting compost, moist peat and grit. If the sink is deep, increase the amount of drainage material. Where lime-hating plants are being used, check that the compost does not contain chalk.

At this stage, a few large rocks can be placed on the soil; bury and incline at a slight angle. Add more compost to within 2.5cm/1in of the rim. Plants can then be put in place, after which add a 12mm/½in-thick layer of rock chippings or pea shingle. The compost will settle, so be prepared to add more surface material later.

Plants for stone sinks

The range of plants is wide and while some, such as conifers, create height, other rock garden plants are small. Spring-flowering dwarf bulbs create

▲ *Miniature hedges help to create an attractive frill for patios, especially when combined with flowering plants such as herbaceous perennials.*

▲ *Stone sinks create homes for hardy, succulent plants such as houseleeks. By leaving plants in their pots the display can be quickly changed.*

bright but diminutive, dainty features.

✹ Spring-flowering bulbs – they include *Crocus chrysanthus* with golden-yellow, goblet-shaped flowers in late winter and early spring, also available in white, blue and purple; *Cyclamen coum* with pink and carmine flowers from mid-winter to early spring; *Eranthis hyemalis* with lemon-yellow flowers backed by light green ruffs during late winter and spring; *Iris danfordiae* with honey-scented, lemon-yellow flowers during mid- and late winter; *Iris reticulata* with bluish-purple flowers with orange blazes in late winter and early spring; *Narcissus bulbocodium* with yellow, hoop-like flowers during late winter and early spring; and *Narcissus cyclamineus* with yellow, narrow trumpets with swept-back petals in late winter and early spring.

✹ Rock garden perennials – *Antennaria rosea* has deep pink flowers during spring and early summer; *Campanula cochleariifolia* has blue bells from mid-

summer to autumn; *Edraianthus pumilio* has lavender-blue flowers from late spring to mid-summer; *Erinus alpinus* has bright pink flowers from early spring to late summer; *Lewisia cotyledon* has pink flowers with white veins during late spring and early summer; and *Saxifraga burseriana* has white flowers during late winter and early spring.

✹ Miniature and slow-growing conifers – plant these while still small and be prepared to remove them when too large. Position tall ones at one end of the sink, with sprawling types at the other because they help to create height and shape.

STAR PLANTS

| Crocus chrysanthus | Eranthis hyemalis |

easy-reach gardens

In an easy-reach garden the planting areas must be accessible and high enough to be reached without bending – high-sided containers and raised beds are ideal. Allowing plenty of space and all-round access to the growing areas will ensure that these gardens can be used by everyone.

◀ *Strategically placed planters help add variety in a paved area, and the plants in them are readily accessible.*

Key features

Many of the features of a garden that's easy to get at make it simple to maintain, and suitable for weekend gardeners or people who haven't got much time to spend on the garden. The only point to bear in mind is that if you use containers as an alternative to raised beds they will need more watering in dry weather. A formal design best suits the requirements of gardens in this group as there needs to be a good deal of uncluttered open space. As a lawn for such areas demands too much attention and upkeep the wise solution is to use a hard, non-slip surface. This can be stone or stone substitute paving, brickwork, brick pavers, or rolled gravel, and the choice will depend partly on the style of the house and also on the budget available. It's worth investing in what you really want as this element of the garden is very visible at all times of year and will also have a very long life.

Except in a very small garden it's usually more effective to vary the surface material, either as an all-over pattern or by using different materials in different areas, or the overall effect can be municipal and monotonous.

Practical considerations

Except where they can be reached from all sides, raised beds or planting containers should be narrow enough for easy access (maximum depth 1.5m/5ft). The sides of a raised bed could also incorporate a seat and if let into the bed this could be used as a place to work on the plants as well as from which to enjoy them. Built features that create maximum effect, such as a rose arch or a long pergola, also provide a visually appealing way of growing plants that require little attention. You might also want to install a formal pool, with wide built-up sides deep enough to provide seating.

For watering, if you can afford the original investment, a built-in irrigation

▲ Setting seats into the raised beds will allow you somewhere to relax and enjoy the plants.

system in the form of a seep hose will be a wonderful aid. If not, the siting of the water supply needs careful consideration. It might be better to have more than one tap, connected to short hoses, than to install one long hose.

With so much hard-landscaping it's a good idea to introduce softer material for elements. Instead of being built in brick, raised beds can be framed in timber, which should be pressure treated to give it the longest possible life and used in conjunction with heavy-duty plastic sheeting to line the inside of the walls and to retain the soil. A seat with an adjacent bench at the right height to be used as a work top while you are sitting would also be a useful feature for this kind of garden.

children's activity gardens

A garden to be used by children should be a happy, fuss-free place. There is no point in cherishing delicate flowers and coddling tall-stemmed beauties here. Eve your velvet lawn will have to be put on hold for now, as a much-used football pit or mountain bike track is seldom smooth and green.

Blending interests

This doesn't mean that you have to deny yourself the pleasures and attractions of a garden if you have children – in some ways your interests will coincide. Most people want a sitting and eating area close to the house and if this is safely constructed and of ample size, it can double up as a daytime playing area for young children, somewhere they are under your eye or can be seen from the window of a room you frequently use. A small but shady tree makes sure that there won't be too much sun-exposure on sunny days. A safety rail is all that differentiates a play-deck from an adults' barbecue area, and shallow steps down if levels change make good sense for adults who'll be using the area at night.

Rather than having a bald and withered lawn, make over a large area to serious rough and tumble play by using a hard-wearing synthetic play surface. In a

bold, curvy shape this area can later become a green lawn, a huge island bed for grasses or herbaceous plants, or even a garden pond when the children get older. Adventure areas can be created with bought equipment such as slides or

swings, and fantasy areas can be formed from exciting plants chosen for their toughness as well as their ability to create a jungle or savanna environment. People who are good at DIY can make climbing frames and clambering posts,

▶ *A children's garden should be stimulating and colourful; these plastic twists reflect the light and bring colour to the garden even in winter.*

◄ An old-fashioned swing is tucked in a corner, while lawn space allows room for very young children to play.

making sure the timber is smoothly planed and firmly and very deeply set in the ground.

Safe and sound

Especially if your children are young it's a good idea to fence your garden in securely so that you know they're safe. Plastic coated mesh fencing is fine for this, taking up minimal space and letting through light for the plants, and it can easily be hidden by climbing plants. A sturdy, child-proof gate is also a must. A soft ground surface is a good idea for adventure areas and a layer of finely shredded bark laid about 15cm/6in thick over a weed-proof membrane is economical for this. Water is such a danger where there are young children that it is much better not to have a garden pond or permanent paddling pool, however much fun and interest these can offer. Instead use an inflatable

▶ Encourage your children to catch the gardening bug by allowing them a small plot of their own in which to grow plants or vegetables.

paddling pool that is only brought out when someone is on the spot to supervise its use.

If your garden has a suitably strong tree it will be tempting to install a tree house despite the cost, and these are increasingly appreciated and used by adults too. At ground level, instead of installing a permanent play house (costs money, takes up space), make sure that there is an open area that can be used for making a tent or wigwam, which will be altogether much better for constructive child development. And if you have a

sandpit make sure it's high-sided to keep the sand in – and remember the cat. Even if you have no cat yourself neighbouring cats will enjoy this giant litter tray. This is not only unpleasant but also potentially a source of disease, so keep the sand pit safely covered when it's not in use.

Finally, many children have strong gardening instincts. If this is the case with your child, the thing to do is to select a small area where he or she can make their own garden. Find a position in the sun where many easy annuals and vegetables will grow well, and not too far from the water supply so that watering will not be difficult.

vegetables and herbs

Few activities in a garden create such a feeling of well-being and self-satisfaction as growing vegetables. Similarly, a herb garden — perhaps in a special bed, in pots near a kitchen door or more decoratively in a bed shaped like a cartwheel — will help to provide additional flavours for meals. A few herbs have an annual nature but many, such as mint, lemon balm, fennel and tarragon, die down during autumn and appear again in spring.

kitchen gardens

There's no denying that growing vegetables, herbs, and maybe some fruit for the kitchen takes time and trouble. But this is more than compensated for by the pleasure it gives. This is an orderly way of gardening that many people find not only intensely rewarding, but also very relaxing.

Planning and preparing

To get the best out of the soil you need to grow vegetables in rotation, and you also need plenty of access to tend and harvest the plants. For these reasons

separate, rectangular plots divided by narrow paths work well. However, if you prefer a more informal design with curves you can still move your vegetables around from area to area. In this case, make sure that your design allows you easy access to the plants.

For the kitchen garden there are three main types of vegetable crop to be planned for: root vegetables (beetroot, carrots, turnips, radishes), brassicas (cabbages and kale) and legumes (peas and beans). The onion family can be given a permanent plot or can be moved along with the legumes. Leeks, going in at a different time from most other vegetables, can be put in as and where there is space. They are planted out in summer, and are finished with by the following spring, leaving the ground free for something else. Lettuces can be planted with the roots or legumes and can also go in as 'catch crops', to be

◀ *This formally laid-out kitchen garden has raised beds which help to provide good drainage and warm the soil.*

removed and eaten as their neighbours grow and need the space.

Preparing the plot

Vegetables are greedy feeders, so the soil needs to be well prepared before you plant. Ideally you should dig it over well in the autumn before you begin and lay a thick layer of manure or garden

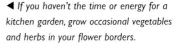

◄ *If you haven't the time or energy for a kitchen garden, grow occasional vegetables and herbs in your flower borders.*

compost on top (or dig it in); then fork over again in the spring. Finally, rake the beds smooth and level to prepare them for seeds and seedlings.

Reasons for rotating

One reason for moving types of crop from area to area is that it discourages the build-up of pests and diseases. There is something nasty specific to almost anything you may wish to grow, and such diseases and predators are much less likely to get established if the crop varies from year to year.

Different types of vegetables also have different requirements, as well as having different effects on the soil. Peas and beans enrich the soil with nitrogen, which is needed by brassicas and leafy vegetables, while root crops help to make the soil comfortable for the legumes. Root crops do best where manure was applied for the previous growing season. Too rich a soil makes them fork under the ground and produce leaf instead of root.

In a big garden, as well as providing beds for three main crop types, you might plan to have a fourth plot for potatoes, which do best on freshly manured soil and which would go around in rotation preceding the root vegetables. Home-grown potatoes are delicious and justify the room – and the work – they take, but not everyone has space to grow and store them in quantity. You could grow a few choice potatoes with the roots and use another area as a permanent site for soft fruits – equally rewarding and worthwhile. You can then pick them at the peak of perfection.

◄ *A well-stocked kitchen garden with ornamental herbs and vegetables provides a feast for the eye as well as for the table.*

herb gardens

Herbs include annuals such as basil that die at the end of summer and perennials such as lemon balm, fennel and tarragon that die down over the winter but grow up again each spring. A few shrubby herbs such as bay, rosemary and thyme flourish during the winter and are available fresh at any time.

Growing herbs together

A well-structured herb garden is a highly ornamental feature in its own right, capable of occupying a defined part of a large garden, or, planned with care, of making an appealing garden in itself. Herbs are used both to flavour food and as medicine, often both at the same time, and they can also be used in a variety of other traditional ways. They offer a rich variety of scents and textures and a herbarium, as the herb garden was once called, is a place to delight the senses. Many herbal plants come from the broad family known as the labiates and the lippy flowers are a magnet to bees so that the garden hums in summer. If you have an interest in history or folklore you may well be lured by the charms of a herb garden and will find yourself making pot pourri and herbal wine as well as using the leaves or flowers in cooking and for herbal teas.

Although there are herbs for a variety of situations and soils many herbs are of Mediterranean origin and need well-drained soil with sun and shelter. Some cultivars with unusual golden or variegated colouring, such as gold-leaf forms of sage or lemon balm thrive if given shade from the summer sun at its

◄ *The plants in your herb garden can be used for home remedies as well as home cooking, and can be dried for winter.*

▶ *Cobbles set in concrete surrounding a small water feature are a strong design focus of this formally laid-out herb garden.*

strongest. Many aromatics actually prefer soil that is not too fertile.

The garden design

Traditionally, herb gardens have been planned rather in the same way as rose gardens (see pages 18–19) with small plots arranged within a formal, geometric structure, each bed enclosed by a low hedge of clipped box. The geometry and formality are complemented by the use of gravel, brick or stone paving for paths and the whole is intricately ornamental. Herbs growing in beds without an enclosure can spill out onto the hard surface for a more informal look, and they also take very well to being planted in containers, which can be used to give more height. Either of these treatments can work well for a patio garden.

While a symmetrical plan based on mirrored beds within a square or rectangle can look over-designed in a smaller garden, the formality of straight-edged planting areas, evergreen edging and hard surfaces can be adapted in many ways to produce a garden with a true herbarium appeal but without the over-demanding symmetry. This sort of solution is particularly suitable for an irregularly shaped plot. The materials used for the hard landscaping of the garden should be in sympathy with the house.

It's worth remembering that a highly formalized herb garden with clipped hedging needs to be kept constantly manicured to look at its best. An informal style can benefit from a slightly negligé look. However you decide to organize your own herb garden, remember that you will need to be able to reach the plants for harvesting, so the depth of bed should not be too great.

◀ *Many herbs lend themselves to a relaxed, informal style of gardening; they look at their best when they are allowed to grow naturally.*

5 7

herb plants and planting

There are dozens of culinary herbs that would grace any garden. And apart from these, herbs in a wider sense include some beautiful and ornamental plants that were once grown for their usefulness, especially in medicine, but which are now known best as garden flowers and shrubs.

Flowers for herb gardens

If you include flowers such as lilies, foxgloves and roses in your herb garden you will be continuing an old apothecary-garden tradition as well as enlivening the garden with spires and mounds of alluring flowers. Selecting widely, you will be able to achieve great variety using only those plants once grown for their use. While it is not advisable to use any of the more powerful plants from the old herbals for self-treatment, growing them to look at is another matter.

As well as the flavouring herbs with which we're still familiar, herbs less widely known, some for kitchen use and some with ancient domestic uses such as keeping away fleas (pennyroyal – a mint) or for making sweetmeats (elecampane), can still be bought from specialist growers. Look out for yellow-headed tansy, blue-leaved rue, red-flowered bergamot and mint-like, blue-flowered hyssop. Add these to the well-known classics such as chamomile, pot marigold, mint, thyme and lavender.

▶ *Rosemary traditionally accompanies lamb and many Mediterranean dishes.*

Profile plants

Rosmarinus officinalis
ROSEMARY

Rosemary makes a lovely shrub with evergreen piney needles and small light blue flowers which may appear from November until early summer.

ht and sp to 1.5m/5ft but can be cut back

Soil and situation

Well-drained soil that is not too rich and a sheltered position in full sun.

Tropaeolum majus
NASTURTIUMS

Nasturtiums are well-loved flowers that bring bright colour to the herb garden. Bushy and climbing varieties are both easily grown from seed.

ht 30cm/12in (bush) 1–3m/3–10ft (climbing)

sp 45cm/18in (bush) 1.2m/4ft (climbing)

Soil and situation

Well-drained soil that is not too rich in a sunny position.

Salvia officinalis
SAGE

Sage makes lovely purple-blue flowers as well as having attractive, felty grey-green leaves. Golden-leaved and purple-leaved varieties are also available ('Aurea' and 'Purpurascens').

ht 75cm/30in

sp 90cm/3ft

Soil and situation

Fairly fertile soil that is light and well-drained, in a sunny position.

▲ *Nasturtiums have edible flowers.*

▲ *Use home-grown sage for Christmas stuffing.*

SOME COMMON HERBS FOR THE KITCHEN

Annual and short-lived herbs

Basil – *Ocimum basilicum*
spicily aromatic, used in pesto and salads; has an affinity with tomatoes.
Dill – *Anethum graveolens*
cool, aromatic flavour blends with fish and potato salad.
Garlic – *Allium sativum*
bulbs have strong piquancy for a Mediterranean flavour.
Parsley ** – *Petroselinum crispum*
indispensable garnishing herb.
Rocket ** – *Eruca sativa*
brings a pungent, peppery flavour to a mixed-leaf salad.

Perennial and shrubby herbs

Bay – *Laurus nobilis*
leathery evergreen leaves for bouquet garni (bay can be grown as topiary).
Chives ** – *Allium schoenoprasum*
onion-flavoured green leaves for garnish; accompanies cream cheese well.
Fennel * – *Foeniculum vulgare*
feathery leaves have a slightly aniseed taste.
French tarragon * – *Artemisia dranunculus*
a subtle aniseed flavour for chicken and sauces.
Marjoram * – *Origanum vulgare*
a good herb for soups, stews and bouquet garni; also for pizza.
Mint ** *Mentha spicata*
well-known cooling and refreshing herb for mint sauce, new potatoes and peas (also known as spearmint), pineapple mint (*M. suaveolens* 'Variegata'), and eau-de-cologne mint (*M.x. piperata* f. *citrata,* syn. M. *citrata*) are some more unusual varieties.
Rosemary * – *Rosmarinus officinalis*
aromatic needles go well with lamb; also for pot pourri and cosmetic uses.
Sage * – *Salvia officinalis*
for pork dishes and sage and onion stuffing.
Salad burnet * – *Poterium sansquisorba*
cucumber-flavoured leaves for salads and summer drinks.
Thyme * – *Thymus vulgaris*
aromatic herb for bouquet garni and to add to soups and stews.

* needs sunshine and good drainage
** needs moisture and semi-shade

▲ *Thyme and the annual basil make an aromatic and decorative combination.*

seasonal displays

The range of plants offered by nurseries and garden centres is amazingly wide and by careful selection spectacular displays can be created throughout the year. Many plants have colourful flowers, while others reveal variegated or single-coloured leaves. Spring is famed for a wealth of bulbs, while summer is awash with the flowers of herbaceous perennials, trees and shrubs. Autumn is known for its glorious berries and several trees have distinctive flowers that survive the bleakness of winter.

spring displays

Bulbs are often thought to signal the start of spring, and several can be used in exciting combinations with shrubs. It is also the time of year when many ornamental cherry trees burst into flower and they too are complemented when underplanted with bulbs, especially daffodils.

Spring-flowering shrubs

One of the most eye-catching shows of yellow is from the bell-shaped flowers of *Forsythia* 'Lynwood'. Like many other spring-flowering shrubs, the flowers appear on naked stems, but the leaves arrive soon after.

Ulex europaeus 'Plenus' (Gorse), is an excellent yellow-flowered evergreen shrub. It has masses of honey-scented, pea-shaped flowers during spring and early summer, and often continues bearing flowers sporadically until the following early spring.

Amelanchier lamarckii (snowy mespilus) is deciduous, with masses of pure-white, star-shaped flowers during mid-spring that never fail to attract attention. *Magnolia stellata* (star magnolia) is smaller, and another white-flowered deciduous shrub. Its individual, 10cm/4in-wide flowers are more dramatic if fewer in number. And *Kerria japonica* 'Pleniflora' (batchelor's buttons) is deciduous, with a lax nature and double, orange-yellow flowers about 5cm/2in wide on slender stems during late spring and early summer. Other spring-flowering shrubs include *Chaenomeles × superba* (flowering quince), *Cytisus × praecox* 'Warminster' (Warminster broom), *Berberis × stenophylla* and *Viburnum × burkwoodii*.

◀ *Colourful spring displays are essential for shedding winter gloom. Prepare for this by planting spring-flowering bulbs in early autumn.*

Spring-flowering bulbs

Some bulbs, such as *Crocus chrysanthus,* which often begins flowering in late winter, can be naturalized in large drifts in short grass, but a more reserved way is to plant groups of spring-flowering bulbs in rock gardens.

Some late winter-flowering bulbs continue their display into early spring and include the pale blue *Chionodoxa luciliae* (glory of the snow), yellow *Eranthis hyemalis* (winter aconite) and white *Galanthus nivalis* (common snowdrop). Others concentrate their flowering in spring and range from *Ipheion uniflorum* (spring starflower), with white to violet-blue, star-shaped flowers, to *Scilla bifolia* (squill) with mauve-blue, white or pink flowers. Two species of tulips for spring include *Tulipa tarda*, with clusters of white flowers that reveal bright yellow centres, and *Tulipa kaufmanniana* (waterlily tulip) that produces star-shaped white flowers flushed red and yellow on the outside.

STAR PLANTS

Amelanchier lamarckii

Clematis montana

Crocus chrysanthus

Eranthis hyemalis

Kerria japonica 'Pleniflora'

Magnolia stellata

Muscari armeniacum

▶ Kerria japonica *'Pleniflora' (bachelor's buttons) creates a superb display in late spring and early summer, with orange-yellow flowers.*

Mixing and matching

As spring progresses there is increasing opportunity to create attractive combinations of plants in borders and against walls. One of these wall-brighteners is *Rosa* 'Helen Knight', (still widely known as *Rosa ecae* 'Helen Knight'), planted alongside the scented *Clematis montana* 'Elizabeth', a variety of the mountain clematis. The rose has fern-like leaves and lightly scented, clear yellow single flowers during late spring, while the clematis bears an abundance of pale pink flowers.

Viburnum opulus 'Roseum' (snowball tree), is a deciduous shrub with large, globular, creamy white flowerheads during late spring and early summer. The branches often bow under the weight of the magnificent flowers. For contrast, plant the herbaceous *Hosta sieboldiana* around its edges.

summer displays

The wealth of colour in summer is almost overwhelming. Herbaceous perennials, hardy and half-hardy annuals, and bulbs create excellent displays, while climbers and wall shrubs cover walls, trellises and pergolas with bright flowers. Variegated and coloured foliage is also a key ingredient.

▲ *Light-faced lilies, with their distinctive shapes, create beacons of brightness in informal borders and are ideal for cottage gardens.*

Summer-flowering shrubs

The wide and varied choice includes early summer-flowering shrubs such as *Cistus × cyprius*, with 7.5cm/3in-wide white flowers blotched crimson, and *Cistus × purpureus* which has rose to purple flowers blotched dark maroon. *Potentilla fruticosa*, a deciduous shrub with many varieties in colours from yellow to bright vermilion, continues its display into late summer. The glorious philadelphus shrubs will enrich any garden in early and mid-summer. Many are richly scented, and there are varieties to suit small gardens.

With the onset of mid-summer many hydrangeas burst into flower. *Hydrangea macrophylla* forms a rounded

STAR PLANTS

Hydrangea macrophylla

Hypericum 'Hidcote'

Laburnum × watereri 'Vossii'

Philadelphus coronarius 'Aureus'

Potentilla fruticosa

Senecio brachyglottis 'Sunshine'

shrub with flowers heads up to 20cm/8in wide. These shrubs have the bonus of flowers into early autumn. Late summer sees other hydrangeas bursting into colour, none more spectacular than *Hydrangea paniculata* 'Grandiflora', with plume-like heads up to 45cm/18in long, packed with white flowers into early autumn.

Mixing and matching

Opportunities abound during summer to mix plants in colourful combinations. For an extra bright display, plant *Genista cinerea*, a large deciduous shrub with yellow, sweetly scented flowers during early and mid-summer, with the evergreen shrub *Brachyglottis* 'Sunshine', still better known as *Senecio* 'Sunshine'. It has grey, white-felted leaves and yellow daisy-like flowers.

The deciduous tree *Laburnum × watereri* 'Vossii' (golden chain tree) is known for its long, pendulous clusters of yellow flowers and forms a background colour contrast with purple lilac.

In wild gardens, the late spring and early summer yellow-flowered deciduous shrub *Rhododendron luteum* has sweet and honey-scented flowers. Plant it alongside a stream, with a dense planting of red variety of *Primula japonica* in front of it. Both thrive under a light canopy of deciduous trees. The evergreen shrub *Rosmarinus officinalis* (rosemary), with grey-green leaves and flowers that mainly appear in spring, then sporadically through to the autumn, is ideal near yellow-leaved *Philadelphus coronarius* 'Aureus'.

Lilies for summer colour

Lilies are popular and are especially attractive when grouped with other plants. Look for *Lilium candidum* (madonna lily) with white, trumpet-shaped flowers during early and mid-summer. Their centres have golden pollen. They are superb when highlighted against a background of the deciduous shrub *Cotinus coggygria* 'Royal Purple', with dark plum-purple leaves. For a less dramatic display, plant the lilies in combination with foxgloves (*Digitalis purpurea*) and a background of blue delphiniums. *Lilium regale* also has white flowers, with their exteriors shaded rose-purple. It creates a rustic and subtle combination with silver birches and ferns such as *Dryopteris filix–mas*.

▲ Plants with all-green or variegated leaves create interest throughout summer. Additionally, they help to suppress the growth of weeds.

COLOURFUL LEAVES

Aucuba japonica 'Variegata' – evergreen shrub with green leaves spotted yellow.

Cotinus coggygria 'Royal Purple' – deciduous shrub with dark plum-purple leaves.

Elaeagnus pungens 'Maculata' – evergreen shrub with green leaves splashed gold.

Humulus lupulus 'Aureus' – yellow-leaved hop, an herbaceous climber with rich yellow leaves.

Philadelphus coronarius 'Aureus' – deciduous shrub with yellow leaves.

Prunus cerasifera 'Pissardii' – deciduous tree with dark red young leaves that turn deep purple as they mature.

Robinia pseudoacacia 'Frisia' – deciduous tree with yellow leaves.

autumn displays

Autumn is thought to be a dull period in the garden, but it is full of colourful flowers, and leaves that turn yellow, orange, gold and red before falling. And even where the flowers of herbaceous plants have turned brown, they look attractive when laced with dew-drenched spiders' webs.

Autumn-flowering shrubs and trees

Several shrubs that flower in late summer continue their display into autumn. They include the magnificent *Buddleia davidii* (butterfly bush) with long, tapering spires of lilac-purple, honey and musk-scented flowers from mid-summer to mid-autumn. There are several varieties in white, deep violet and lavender-blue. *Caryopteris ×*

clandonensis (bluebeard) has aromatic grey-green leaves and blue flowers from late summer, while *Hibiscus syriacus* (shrubby mallow) bears trumpet-shaped flowers from mid-summer to early autumn, in colours including violet-blue and rose-pink.

The popular *Hydrangea macrophylla* (common hydrangea) is bushy with large, mainly blue flower-heads that continue

into autumn. Another magnificent summer and autumn-flowering shrub is *Lavatera* 'Rosea', (tree mallow), also known as *Lavatera olbia* 'Rosea'. The branching stems bear masses of rose-coloured flowers.

Glorious corms

These are often associated with bulbs but instead of having an onion-like structure, their stem bases are greatly swollen. *Crocus longiflorus* has goblet-shaped, lilac and deep bluish-mauve flowers with prominent orange stigmas and orange feathering in the throat during mid- and late autumn. And *C. sativus* (saffron crocus), has red-purple flowers, large red stigmas and orange stamens during mid-autumn. A more popular and hardier corm is *Cyclamen hederifolium*, with flowers in a range of colours from white, through pale pink to mauve, from late summer to late autumn.

Lilies for autumn colour

Several summer-flowering lilies continue their display into autumn and are

▲ *The leaves of the deciduous shrub* Rhus typhina *(stag's horn sumach) turn brilliant shades of orange-red, yellow and purple.*

welcome for the stately appearance of their flowers, but they need a sunny and wind-sheltered position. *Lilium auratum* (golden-rayed lily) has sweetly scented, funnel-shaped, brilliant white flowers during late summer and early autumn. Each flower has a golden-yellow ray or band. *L. henryi* also has sweetly scented flowers, but they are pale apricot-yellow with red spots, again during late summer and early autumn. More popular is *L. speciosum* (Japanese lily) with white, partly crimson-shaded flowers.

STAR PLANTS

Buddleia davidii	Hydrangea macrophylla
Hibiscus syriacus	Lavatera 'Rosea'

Mixing and matching

Create a late summer display that, in part, continues to mid-autumn or later by planting the 90cm/3ft-high, rose 'Ophelia' with blush-pink flowers among the sky blue, trumpet-like flowers of the early to late autumn-flowering *Gentiana sino-ornata*. It grows about 15cm/6in high with a 30–38cm/12–15in spread. The rose continues flowering into early autumn, especially in mild areas. For a richer colour scheme plant a row of *Sedum* 'Autumn Joy', now known as *Sedum* 'Herbstfreude'. It bears slightly domed heads packed with salmon-pink flowers that slowly change through orange-red to orange-brown in mid- and late autumn.

▲ *Massed hydrangeas create dominant features from mid-summer to early auumn. Additionally, the old flower-heads look very attractive when covered in frost.*

SHRUBS AND TREES WITH AUTUMN-COLOURED LEAVES

Hamamelis mollis (Chinese witch hazel) – sharp yellow

Liquidambar styraciflua (sweet gum) – rich orange and scarlet shades

Koelreuteria paniculata (golden rain tree) – rich yellow

Malus tschonoskii – rich red and yellow

Parrotia persica – crimson, gold and amber tints

Rhus typhina (stag's horn sumac) – rich orange-red, purple and yellow tints

winter displays

Corners of gardens devoted to winter-flowering plants create oases of interest when the garden might otherwise be lacking colour. Apart from winter flowers, many shrubs and trees have wonderfully coloured stems or bark. Some make excellent focal points.

Winter-flowering shrubs and trees

These create a permanent framework around which other plants can be positioned. Many have scented flowers and they include *Hamamelis mollis* (Chinese witch hazel) and *Hamamelis japonica* (Japanese witch hazel), both with spider-like flowers borne on naked branches. *Viburnum × bodnantense* 'Dawn' reveals sweetly scented white flowers, flushed red, from early to late winter, and *V. farreri* bears white flowers over a similar period. Richly coloured mahonias are also evident in winter, and few compare with the evergreen *Mahonia × media* 'Charity'. It has tapering spires of sweetly scented, yellow flowers from late autumn to late winter.

Glorious bulbs

Some winter-flowering bulbs are slightly variable in the exact time they flower, often blooming on the cusp of late winter and early spring, depending on the weather. The rich golden-yellow, goblet-like flowers of *Crocus chrysanthus* always get plenty of attention. They flower during late winter into early spring, and are superb in a rock garden or when naturalized around a silver birch. The slightly earlier flowering *Iris reticulata* (netted iris) creates a feast of violet-scented, deep blue-purple flowers each with an orange blaze during mid- and late winter. Its diminutive nature, about 10cm/4in high, makes it ideal for a rock garden or the edge of a path. *I. histrioides* 'Major' bears rich blue flowers at about the same time and looks good in a medley of golden crocuses and especially white *Galanthus nivalis* (snowdrops), an essential part of the winter garden. During mid- and late winter it bears white nodding flowers, some slightly scented.

▲ *The diminutive and bulbous-rooted* Iris reticulata *'Harmony' produces a wealth of flowers. It is ideal for planting in a rock garden.*

Mixing and matching

Here are a couple of rich associations with the added benefit of scented flowers. First, try *Helleborus niger* (Christmas rose) around the early to late winter flowering shrub *Chimonanthus praecox* 'Grandiflorus' (winter sweet). The hellebore has saucer-shaped white flowers, while the winter sweet reveals spicily scented, claw-like flowers formed of yellow outer petals and red centres. The second plant association is *Hamamelis mollis* (Chinese witch hazel), with rich golden-yellow, spider-like flowers in midwinter, and an underplanting of the yellow-green evergreen shrub *Euonymus japonicus* 'Viridivariegatus'. A few plants of the low-growing evergreen shrub *Sarcococca confusa* (Christmas box), with white, sweetly scented flowers, add further colour contrasts.

ATTRACTIVE BARK

Many trees have distinctive coloured bark that is especially welcome in winter.

Acer griseum (paperbark maple) – Buff-coloured bark that peels to reveal orange-brown under-bark.

Acer pensylvanicum (snakebark maple) – trunk and branches with jagged white lines.

Arbutus × andrachnoides – cinnamon-red bark.

Betula utilis 'Jaquemontii' – peeling bark, usually white but light pinkish-brown and ochre-cream forms are available.

▶ *Shrubs with coloured stems in winter always attract attention. Here is the thicket-forming Cornus alba 'Sibirica', with bright crimson stems. It is ideal for planting alongside streams.*

STAR PLANTS

Hamamelis mollis

Mahonia × media 'Charity'

Crocus chrysanthus

Chimonanthus praecox

Jasminum nudiflorum

Sarcococca confusa

COLOURED STEMS

If these suckering shrubs are radically pruned to near soil level in the spring, they develop attractive young stems during summer that colour up for winter.

Cornus alba (red-barked dogwood) – rich red stems.

Cornus alba 'Sibirica' (Westonbirt dogwood) – brilliant crimson stems.

Cornus stolonifera (red osier dogwood) – dull red stems.

Cornus stolonifera 'Flaviramea' (dogwood) – bright yellow to olive-green stems.

◀ *The hardy, evergreen shrub* Mahonia x media *'Charity' never fails to create a dominant display of yellow flowers in winter.*

plant directory

Within this information-packed chapter there are plants that will help you create your desired garden, whether it has a relaxed cottage style or is formal and with geometrically shaped and regularly arranged flower beds. The plants in this comprehensive directory are arranged under their type, such as annuals and biennials, bulbous, herbaceous perennials and so on. Within each entry information is given about the plant's size, range of colour and desired soil and aspect.

plant directory

ANNUALS AND BIENNIALS

Annuals and biennials are short-lived plants usually grown for one season only. After flowering they die down and only rarely survive the winter. Annuals come into flower within 12 months of the seed being sown. Biennials usually flower in the second flowering season of their lives. Both can be raised quite easily from seed and bring colour and variety to the garden.

Alcea rosea
(syn. *Althaea rosea*)
HOLLYHOCK

Hollyhocks are lovely old-fashioned flowers with large rosettes or (in the double form) pompons of flowers towering above the leaves in spires, best grown as a biennial although they may last. The flowers come in a range of colours which all blend well together, from deep crimson, maroon and violet purple to white, pink and chalky yellow. A real cottage garden plant, hollyhocks grow quite happily against a house wall or through cracks in paving and also look good in a sunny border where their height can be appreciated. They flower from later summer onward, attracting butterflies and bees. *A. r.* 'Chater's Double' (tall) and *A. r.* 'Majorette' (short) are double forms, the latter flowering a little earlier and being particularly good in a mixed grouping.
ht 1.8m/6ft or more (tall), 60–90 cm/2–3ft (short)
sp 60cm/2ft
Soil and position
For well-drained and even stony, but fertile, soils in a light, sunny position. In all but sheltered places they will need staking.

Bassia scoparia
(syn. *Kochia scoparia*)
SUMMER CYPRESS
OR BURNING BUSH

This green-leaved bedding plant looks like a miniature conifer, adding shape and solidity to a planting scheme. Well used it can be a useful foliage plant, bringing a temporary mound of bright new green into the garden. You can grow it in a pot instead of topiary, or line the plants up to make a summer-long 'hedge'. In the autumn it colours up to a glowing bronze-red before succumbing to harsh weather. A non-reddening variety, 'Evergreen' is also available.
ht 90cm/3ft
sp 45cm/18in
Soil and position
Almost any, though light soil and open position are best.

Bellis perennis
BACHELOR'S BUTTON

Bachelor's buttons are little garden daisies that flower in late spring in shades of pink, red and white – some bi-coloured, and each with a yellow centre. Grow these neat little plants as a biennial from seed the previous summer, or buy as small plants. 'Carpet Mixed' and Pomponette Series are a good choice.
ht to 20cm/8in
sp 15cm/6in
Soil and position
Well-drained soil in sun or partial shade.

Brachyscome iberidifolia
SWAN RIVER DAISY

The Swan River daisy produces masses of daisy-like flowers in shades of blue or pinkish purple, sometimes with an inner ring of white. Can be grown easily from seed sown in spring but does best in a sunny spot. In warm, sheltered places it will even seed itself into cracks in stone walls. Good for hanging baskets and

◄ Alcea rosea (syn. Althaea rosea) hollyhock.

containers; flowers from early to late summer.

ht 23–45cm/9–18in
sp 30cm/12in
Soil and position
Very well-drained soil in a sunny, sheltered position.

Calendula
CALENDULA

Calendula or pot marigold is a good old-fashioned garden flower, easily grown from seed. The bright orange petals of the plant originally grown in plots and gardens, *C. officinalis*, were dried and used in winter stews. There are now many attractive cultivars in shades of bright orange, orange-yellow and cream, with lance-shaped, pale green leaves. *C. officinalis* Pacific Beauty Series includes a large, warm yellow marigold with the name 'Yellow Queen' as well as many others with unusual and subtle shades.

ht 30–60cm/12–24in
sp 30–45cm/12–18in

Soil and position
Likes even poor soil, as long as it's well-drained, and seeds itself merrily in a warm, sunny position.

Centaurea cyanus
CORNFLOWER

The familiar cornflower is at home in informal schemes and will flower for a long period as long as you cut off stems as the flowers die. Seeds can be sown in spring but the plants are stronger and earlier to flower if you start them off the previous autumn. Mixed shades of pink, white and purple are available as well as the original blue. Can be grown in pots or containers for a patio display. Need the support of twiggy sticks in less sheltered positions.

ht 20–75cm/8–30in
sp 15cm/6in
Soil and position
Do best in ordinary well-drained soil and good light. Will tolerate some drought.

Clarkia
CLARKIA AND GODETIA

Easy plants to grow from seed, *Clarkia elegans* or clarkia has cheerful, salmon-pink flowers bustling up the stems (also purple and lavender pink shades). *C. amoena* or *godetia* has silky, tissue-papery, more delicate flowers, mainly in shades of pink and white, some with interesting markings. All flower during the main summer months after a spring sowing outdoors. An autumn sowing will produce earlier-flowering plants the following year. (*Clarkia elegans* is now properly called *Clarkia unguiculata* but the name is not widely in use.)

ht 30–90cm/12–36in depending on variety
sp 20–30cm/8–12in
Soil and position
Clarkias need well-drained, slightly acid soil with protection from full sun – often flower best in dry, poor soil.

Consolida ajacis
LARKSPUR

Larkspur, the poor man's delphinium, has flowery spikes of spurred flowers in blue or mixed shades of pink, ruby red, white and violet, and finely cut leaves. This plant is very much at home in an informal border. The seeds can be sown in the open in early

▲ *Centaurea cyanus or cornflower, ideal for informal gardens.*

spring and the plant will usually self-seed. Giant Imperial Series are particularly strong and well-branched.

ht 90cm/3ft (dwarf varieties 30cm/12in)
sp 25cm/10in
Soil and position
Undemanding as to soil, as long as it is well drained.
CAUTION: LARKSPUR SEEDS ARE POISONOUS.

Cosmos bipinnatus 'Sensation Mixed'
COSMOS OR COSMEA

The airy, daisy-like flowers of cosmos have a delicacy that is enhanced by their feathery foliage, and the plants flower from mid- to late summer until the first frosts from seed sown indoors in spring. The common variety 'Sensation Mixed' produces tall flowers in white and lilac-y pinks and purples. Individual shades are available from within the Sensation Series.

ht 90cm/3ft
sp 45cm/18in
Soil and position
Reasonably fertile, moist but well-drained soil and a sunny position.

Dianthus barbatus
SWEET WILLIAM

There are many garden dianthus, including pinks and carnations.

◀ *The purple flowers of the Swan River daisy, Brachyscome iberidifolia.*

▲ Salvia splendens, *salvia, flowers throughout the summer.*

D. barbatus are the fuzzy, bright-coloured sweet williams that have an old-fashioned appeal and are best grown as biennials from seed sown early the previous summer and planted out in autumn, or bought as bedding plants in spring. There are many varieties. Most are banded or bi-coloured with a central eye and have a sweet scent. Cutting the plants back after the first flowering early in the summer will usually encourage a second crop of flowers. Plants can be left to chance their luck over the winter and may develop into good clumps in the right soil conditions.
ht 45cm/18in
sp 25cm/10in
Soil and position
Well-drained, fertile soil, preferably slightly alkaline, and a bright, sunny position.

Digitalis purpurea
FOXGLOVE
Foxgloves need no introduction.

Grouped together in a semi-shady spot they add tranquillity to any garden, and of course are useful for their height as well. As well as the purple shade that gives the plant its name, foxgloves now come in shades of cream, apricot and pink. Excelsior Hybrids are in shades that blend well together and are tall-growing. *D. g.* f. *albiflora* is a pure white-flowered form. Because of their height they need staking in all but the most sheltered spots.
ht to 2m/6ft 6in
sp to 60cm/24in
Soil and position
Tolerate all but extremes but prefer humus-rich soil and dappled shade. They are excellent in light woodland, and will seed themselves where suited.
CAUTION: ALL PARTS OF THE PLANT CAN BE HARMFUL IF EATEN.

Erysimum cheiri
(syn. *Cheiranthus cheiri*)
WALLFLOWER
It would be hard to manage without this beautifully scented bedding plant in late spring. The flowers may be simple and not very large but the velvety petals have wonderfully intense colours, from deep blood red and crimson to bright eggyolk yellow. The single-coloured varieties 'Blood Red' and 'Cloth of Gold' speak for themselves, and 'Persian Carpet' gives a good mixture of shades. They can be grown from seed sown the previous spring but are readily available as young plants in late autumn. Plant close together for the best effect. *E.* 'Bowles Mauve' is an evergreen perennial, but without the wallflower scent. It flowers throughout the year.
ht to 45cm/18in
sp to 30cm/12in

▶ Helianthus annuus, *annual sunflower.*

Soil and position
Well-drained, fertile, fairly alkaline soil in a bright position.

Euphorbia marginata
GHOST WEED
Also known as 'snow-on-the-mountain', this hardy annual euphorbia adds a touch of class. Although the plant does flower, its white-marked foliage is what appeals. Given the right position it will flourish all summer grown from a spring planting outdoors. It's also a good plant for patio pots or containers.
ht 60–90 cm/ 2–3 ft
sp 30 cm/ 12 in
Soil and position
Needs a light, well-drained soil and an open, sunny position.
CAUTION: THE SAP CAN CAUSE SEVERE IRRITATION TO THE SKIN.

Gomphrena globosa
GLOBE AMARANTH
Globe amaranth is unusual and colourful and fairly undemand-ing. Its robust clover-shaped flowers come in shades of red and pink; its bushy shape makes

it a good border filler. The flowers can be dried for indoor use. Flowers all summer from seeds sown indoors in spring.
ht 30–60cm/1–2ft
sp 40cm/10in
Soil and position
Needs well-drained, fairly fertile soil and a sunny position.

Helianthus annuus
ANNUAL SUNFLOWER
In recent years many new forms of the cottage garden sunflower have been produced, so dwarf plants as well as towering giants are available. Flowers are in shades of yellow and orange and the central disc develops into the heavy seedhead which will attract birds when ripened. 'Pacino' is a good reliable, traditional variety; dwarf varieties include 'Music Box' and 'Teddy Bear'.
ht to 5m/15ft (tall); 45cm/18in (dwarf); 70cm/28in ('Music Box'); 90cm/36in ('Teddy Bear')
sp to 60cm/2ft
Soil and conditions
Well-drained, humus-rich soil,

including alkaline soil and soil that is fairly dry. The plants need a warm summer to do well.

Ipomoea
MORNING GLORY

Morning glory is an annual climber with twining stems to be grown from seed sown in late spring. It has heart-shaped leaves and singly borne flowers in flattened trumpet shapes, wide and flaring, usually in a bright, clear blue. Each one lasts only a day, but the plant is covered with flowers all summer. A few plants together will quickly grow up a fence or climb up a wigwam. The variety *Ipomoea purpurea* has flowers in pink, pinkish blue, purple and white. *I. tricolor* (syn. *I. violacea*) has white-centred, sky-blue flowers.
ht 3m/10ft
sp 30cm/12in
Soil and position
Well-drained, but fertile soil in a sheltered, sunny position.

Lathyrus odoratus
SWEET PEA

Members of the pea family, sharing the wiry tendrils by which pea plants cling to a support, sweet peas have wavy-edged flowers in a very wide range of pastel colours, with some in bright, deep reds and darkest purple. Not difficult to grow from seed sown outside in the autumn or indoors in late winter or early spring, they can also be bought as small plants in pots in late spring and will flower from early summer until the autumn. Delicious scent (in most varieties) and luscious colours make them delightful cut flowers as well; the more you cut the more the plants produce. Plant out in groups and provide netting, tall twiggy sticks or other supports. 'Jet Set Mixed' and 'Knee High' are dwarf varieties suitable for patio pots.
ht to 2m/6ft 6in to 2.5m/8ft; 1m/39in (dwarf varieties)
sp 15–25cm/6–10in (the plants grow into each other planted at these intervals)
Soil and position
Fertile, deeply dug soil that is moist but well-drained, and a light, sunny, but sheltered position.

▶ Sweet pea, Lathyrus odoratus.

◀ The tobacco plant, Nicotiana, suits well-drained soil in sun or partial shade.

Lavatera trimestris
ANNUAL GARDEN MALLOW

This annual garden mallow makes a shrubby, flowery plant that belies its ease of growth. One of the commonest varieties is the pink-flowering 'Silver Cup', which is showy and cheerful but a bit too pink for some tastes. Try 'Mont Blanc' for a snowy white. Seeds can be sown directly outside in spring.
ht 75cm/30in
sp 40cm/16in
Soil and position
Light, well-drained, fairly fertile soil and a sunny but sheltered position.

Limnanthes douglasii
POACHED EGG PLANT

Poached egg plant forms a low and spreading mass of eggy yellow-centred flowers that are very attractive to bees and hoverflies (which devour greenfly). Flowering in mid-summer, they can be sown in early autumn or mid- to late spring. Where the plant feels at home it will self-seed for the following year.
ht to 23cm/9in
sp 15cm/6in
Soil and position
Needs a well-drained, but fairly moist soil and an open, sunny position.

Lunaria annua
(syn. *Lunaria biennis*)
HONESTY

Also known as 'money plant' because of its round, flat seed-heads, *Lunaria annua* most commonly has purple flowers. *L. a.* var. *albiflora* has white flowers, *L. a.* 'Variegata' has white-splashed leaves, and *L.a.* 'Alba Variegata' is blessed with both. The plant usually self-seeds. Mature plants grow from the seedlings of the previous year's spring sowing.
ht to 90cm/3ft
sp 30cm/12in
Soil and position
No special requirements.

Meconopsis cambrica
WELSH POPPY

Not immediately recognizable as a poppy, Welsh poppy is a bright, clear yellow and somewhat shorter than most annual poppies. It shares the silky petals, hairy stems and nodding flower buds of other poppies and frequently pops up in just the right place. Similar, but even more unusual, is *M. grandis*, the Himalayan poppy, with flowers of a stunning blue.
ht 38cm/15in
sp 20cm/8in
Soil and position
Almost any reasonably well-drained, but not dry, soil in partial shade. Hot dry summers do not suit this plant.

Moluccella laevis
BELLS OF IRELAND

Bells of Ireland has spikes of unusual greenish flowers which can also be dried for winter flower arrangements. What appear to be the flowers are really green calyces that look like elfin caps, almost hiding tiny, slightly scented white flowers. The plant flowers in late summer. Seeds can be sown indoors in early spring or outdoors in late spring, where the plants are to flower.
ht 60–90cm/2–3ft
sp 20cm/8in
Soil and position
Needs fertile, well-drained soil and a sheltered position.

Nemophila menziesii
NEMOPHILA

This is a spreading, low-growing flowering plant for rockeries and border edges. The pretty, light green foliage is almost hidden by the masses of small, pale-blue, white-centred flowers in the best-known variety 'Baby Blue Eyes'. A classy black and white version, 'Penny Black', and the pure white 'Snowstorm' give the gardener plenty of choice. The plants, which flower throughout the summer, can be grown from seed sown outside in late spring.
ht 20cm/8in
sp 30cm/12in
Soil and position
The plants like well-drained, fertile soil but need some moisture, and thrive in part shade as well as full sun.

◀ Nigella damascena, *love-in-a-mist.*

Nicotiana
TOBACCO PLANT

The tobacco plants widely on sale for summer planting are usually Domino Series cultivars and come in various colours from red and deep pink to white, cream and lime green, mauve and purple. These are very cheerful and have some scent, but if fragrance is what you're after the taller *Nicotiana alata* is worth looking out for. The milky white or lime green flowers are especially well scented at night. A rather different species, the tall *N. sylvestris* has heads of strongly scented, pendent flowers, long, narrow and tubular, from branching stems above broad, tobacco leaves. All are normally grown as biennials and flower from early to late summer.
ht 30cm/12in (Domino Series);
2–3ft (N. alata); 4–5ft
(N. sylvestris)
sp 30cm/12in; 60cm/24in
(N. sylvestris)
Soil and position
Fertile, well-drained, moist soil and sun or light shade.
CAUTION: THE FOLIAGE CAN BE A SKIN IRRITANT.

Nigella damascena
LOVE-IN-A-MIST

Love-in-a mist does have a misty look, because of its mass of wispy foliage and misty blue flowers. The inflated seed pods are an extra attraction. This annual is a cottage garden favourite that looks at home in many other situations too. A mixed strain is available in a range of moody blues, pinks and purples, and white (Persian Jewels Series mixed). Purists, however, like to stick with 'Miss Jekyll', in beautiful blue. The seeds are best sown where they are to grow as doesn't like being transplanted.
ht 40–45cm/16–18in
sp 23cm/9in
Soil and position
Moist, fertile, well-drained soil and a sheltered, sunny spot. Does best in fairly cool summers.

Papaver
POPPIES

Every flower garden is enhanced by annual poppies. They have a long flowering season, wave about in the breeze and catch the light beautifully, are tissue-paper fine and fleeting and come in lovely colours. *P. rhoeas* Shirley Series, the Shirley poppy comes in single and double varieties in watercolour shades of pinks, light purple, white, and occasionally orange and red. *P. somniferum*, known as opium poppy, has various shades of sultry pink, purple, and occasionally white or red, and bluish leaves, seedheads and stems.
ht 90cm/3ft (P. rhoeas); to 1.2m/ 4ft (P. somniferum)
sp 30cm/12in
Soil and position
Reasonably fertile, well-drained soil in good light.
CAUTION: POISONOUS IF EATEN.

Rudbeckia hirta
RUDBECKIA

Rudbeckia hirta, sometimes known as coneflower, are perennials that are grown as annuals, casting a warm glow in the garden in later summer and early autumn. The flowers are large, single petalled and daisy-like, in shades of warm yellows, reds and reddish browns, with conical centres of purple-brown, and are borne on sturdy, branching stems with a mass of simple, darkish green leaves. Among the best are 'Rustic Dwarfs' in a good range of dark-zoned and flecked colours; 'Goldilocks, with double or semi-double golden flowers, and

'Marmalade' with large, bright yellow flowers. 'Becky Mixed' is a dwarf variety in a mix of colours. Cut the stems after flowering to prolong the flowering period.

ht 60cm/24in; 25cm/10in
('Becky Mixed')
sp 30–45cm/12–18in
Soil and position
Fertile, well-drained soil and a position in full sun.

Salvia splendens
SALVIA

This is a perennial grown as an annual bedding plant, flowering during the whole summer and surviving even the early frosts. With their vibrant flowers they are widely used in park bedding schemes. There's no need to stick to red salvias as the spikes of tubular flowers now come in a range of pinks, purples and muted orange as well. 'Blaze of Fire' speaks for itself; Cleopatra Series are violet purple; others to choose are *S. s.* 'Phoenix Mixed', *S. s.* ' Phoenix Purple' and 'Sizzler Mixed' in the Sizzler Series.

ht 30–40cm/12–16in
sp 25–30cm/10–12in
Soil and position
Needs a soil with good drainage and a light position with plenty of sunlight.

Scabiosa atropurpurea
SWEET SCABIOUS

Sweet scabious or pincushion flower has lilac blue flowers carried singly on narrow, wiry stems all summer. The loose, wavy petals surround a 'pincushion' centre and the flowers attract butterflies and bees. They are best grown in small groups in an informal border. Short-lived perennials, they are usually treated as a biennial (with seed sown the previous spring) or annual. 'Double Mixed' and 'Dwarf Double Mixed' have flowers in shades of white, pink, and purple, as well as blue.

ht 90cm/36in; 45cm/18in
(dwarf types)
sp 20cm/8in
Soil and position
A well-drained, fertile, limy or even chalky soil is best and an open, sunny position.

Tropaeolum
NASTURTIUM

Nasturtiums are easy annuals that are very well worth growing for their bright, velvety, spurred flowers and round, flat, greyish green (and edible) leaves. Most make bushy, low-growing little plants but some are climbers that quickly scramble up a fence or trellis, or over another plant. Many named hybrids are available, in single colours (scarlet, orange, mahogany, yellow and cream), or with white-splashed leaves. Alaska Series has leaves that are marbled with cream and pink. Look out for blackfly, which tend to gather on the backs of the leaves.

ht 30–60cm/12–24in;
1–3m/3–10ft (climbers)
sp 45–60cm/18–24in
Soil and position
Flower best when grown in poor but well-drained soil, and in a sunny position.

▼ Meconopsis cambrica *'Welsh poppy'*
is small with bright yellow flowers.

◄ Allium christophii, *allium.*

BULBOUS PLANTS

Bulbous plants produce a huge range of flowers, not just in spring but at almost every time of year, and for every situation from well-drained rockeries to moist meadows and pondsides. Allowing the foliage to die down naturally after flowering enables them to build up their resources for the following year, and when they feel at home they thrive. This list includes plants grown from bulbs, corms and rhizomes – all being food-storage organs which enable the plant to survive the dormant period.

Agapanthus africanus
AGAPANTHUS OR
AFRICAN LILY

In late summer agapanthus has drumheads of bell-shaped or trumpet-like flowers on tall, stately stems, usually in shades of blue although some varieties are white. This striking plant has a mass of long, spear-shaped leaves, and is excellent for containers as well as in garden beds. In all but the most mild and sheltered areas needs protecting with a thick mulch in winter.
ht 60–90cm/2–3ft (a few varieties much taller)
sp 45–60cm/18–24in
Soil and position
Must have a light, well-drained but moist soil or potting compost, and needs a very light position.

Allium christophii
ALLIUM

This member of the onion family produces lilac-coloured globes of star-shaped flowers on tall stalks, and strappy grey-green leaves, making an architectural plant. There are many different species of allium, producing flowers from spring to autumn and in a wide range of heights from dainty to stately. *Allium christophii* flowers in early summer. *A. giganteum* is a giant version with dense round heads of purplish flowers in summer.
ht 60cm/2ft (Allium christophii);
1.5–2m/5–6.5ft (A. giganteum)
sp 15cm/6in (both)
Soil and position
Not fussy as to soil, as long as it is fairly well-drained. Needs a sunny position.
CAUTION: THE JUICE FROM THE BULBS CAN CAUSE SKIN ALLERGIES OR A RASH.

Anemone blanda
WINDFLOWER

Flowering in early spring in shades of heavenly blue, bluish pink, pinky purple and pure white, this daisy-like anemone, with its deeply cut leaves, is a lovely plant for a semi-wild 'woodland' area or rock garden, and will soon spread widely if it feels at home.
ht 15cm/6in
sp 10cm/4in
Soil and position
Well-drained soil that is not too dry, in a position in sun or partial shade. Grows well under deciduous trees as it flowers before the leaves open.

Arum italicum
LORDS AND LADIES OR
CUCKOOPINT

Closely related to the wild woodland plant, the garden arum has very glossy leaves in winter and early spring, from the centre of which springs up a sturdy spike of minute flowers surrounded by a sail-like spathe in creamy green. In late summer the spike becomes a head of bright red beady berries. The variety *A.i.* 'Marmoratum' (syn. *A. i.* 'Pictum') has marble-patterned, variegated leaves. The less hardy *Arum pictum* has narrow, white-veined leaves.

ht 30cm/12in
sp 15cm/6in
Soil and position
Humus-rich but well-drained soil in any position from full sun to shade.

Chionodoxa
GLORY OF THE SNOW

In early spring chionodoxa produces bright, wide-open, starry flowers amid shapely mid-green leaves. *Chionodoxa forbesii* (sometimes sold as *C. luciliae*) is the species usually grown; its flowers are a clear blue with white centres, or, in the variety 'Pink Giant', a lovely soft pink. Chionodoxa is a good plant to grow in a rockery or under deciduous trees, where it will seed itself and spread freely.
ht 10–20cm/4–8in
sp 2.5cm/1in
Soil and position
Well-drained soil with adequate moisture, in sun.

Colchicum
COLCHICUM OR
AUTUMN CROCUS

These delicately coloured early autumn-flowering crocus-like plants have acquired the name 'naked ladies' from the fact that their broad, most un-crocus-like leaves appear at a completely different time from the 'naked' flowers. Some are rare and sought-after (and expensive to buy) but *C. autumnale*, the meadow saffron, and *C. speciosum* are both quite widely available. Both come in several varieties, in white and rosy lilac-pink.
ht 10–15cm/4–6in
sp 8cm/3in
Soil and position
Fertile garden soil and an open, sunny position.

Crinum × Powellii
CRINUM

Crinums are lily-like flowers from South Africa and many of them don't like our climate. But *Crinum × Powellii* is surprisingly hardy and bears its hanging pink or white trumpet-shaped flowers well into autumn. Each sturdy stem bears six to eight flowers and the bulbs form clumps, with broad, strap-shaped leaves. Protect with a thick mulch in winter in all but very mild areas.
ht 90cm/3ft
sp 30cm/12in
Soil and position
Well-drained soil, with moisture, and a warm, sheltered spot.
CAUTION: ANY PART OF THE PLANT CAN CAUSE SEVERE STOMACH UPSET; THE JUICES CAN CAUSE SKIN IRRITATION.

Crocus
CROCUS

Spring-flowering crocuses are a must in any garden, planted under trees, in a rockery, or in pots on the patio or corners of the border. Among the earliest to flower are *C. tommasinianus*, in delicate shades of amethyst blue to lilac, and (in 'Ruby Giant') reddish purple. The bolder *C. vernus* comes in the same colour range, including brighter shades, but also in golden yellow ('Dutch Yellow'), and with feathered forms (as in 'Joan of Arc') or stripes ('Winston Churchill'). These usually flower in mid-spring, as does *Crocus angustifolius* or cloth of gold, which has yellow flowers which are bronze-stained on the outside, with a delicate fragrance. The corms soon spread, forming small clumps. Robust forms are good for naturalizing in grass.
ht to 10cm/4in
sp 2.5cm/1in
Soil and position
Well-drained soil and a sunny situation, where they will not be disturbed.

▲ Agapanthus africanus *or African lily.*

Cyclamen coum
CYCLAMEN

This winter-flowering native of northern Turkey will flourish in the shelter of trees and shrubs. Flared-back flowers come in white and shades of pink and purple, and the flat, heart-shaped leaves are very dark green and usually attractively marbled in silver. Flowers continue until mid-spring. Must be bought from a licensed source to ensure that illegally imported, wild corms are not used.
ht 10cm/4in
sp to 15cm/6in
Soil and position
Well-drained, humus-rich soil that does not dry out in summer; sun or partial shade.
CAUTION: ALL PARTS OF THE PLANT CAN CAUSE SEVERE STOMACH UPSET IF EATEN.

◄ Eranthis hyemalis, *winter aconite*
flowers in late winter.

Erythronium dens-canis
DOG'S TOOTH VIOLET

With their backward-flaring
petals and marbled leaves these
little plants look similar to
cyclamen and flower in spring.
The leaves are broad and
pointed, with purplish brown
splodges, and the flowers are in
white, pink or lilac, depending
on the variety. 'Lilac Wonder',
'Pink Perfection', 'Snowflake',
'White Splendour' and 'Purple
King' all live up to their names.
Erythroniums look pretty
growing under trees or shrubs, in
rockeries, or naturalized in the
lawn, and they spread to form
small clumps.
ht and sp 10–15cm/4–6in
Soil and position
Well-drained, humus-rich soil
that does not dry out in summer,
in lightly dappled shade.

Fritillaria imperialis
CROWN IMPERIAL

This is a large and striking
member of the fritillary family,
flowering in late spring. Whorls
of spiky, pale green leaves top the
orange, bell-shaped flowers
clustered at the tops of strong
brown stems. The variety *F. i.*
'Lutea Maxima' has lemon-
yellow flowers.
ht to 1.5m/3–5ft
sp to 90cm/12in
Soil and position
Fertile, well-drained soil in sun
or partial shade.

Galtonia
SUMMER HYACINTH

True to the family they come
from, galtonias look like loose-
flowered hyacinths. The closely
packed buds towards the tops of
the stems open into pendent,
bell-like flowers and the plants
form clumps with wide, strap-
shaped, slightly arching leaves.

Dahlia
DAHLIA

Dahlias jolly up the garden in
late summer and last until the
first frosts. Apart from the
cheerful pompom-headed and
multi-petalled cactus types there
are elegant single flowering
dahlias for those who like
restraint and dwarf dahlias that
don't need staking (as the others
generally do). 'Bishop of
Llandaff' is a peony-flowered
form with brilliant red flowers
and stunning reddish black
foliage; 'Easter Sunday' is a white,
single form with a 'collerette' of
small petals around the central
yellow disc; 'Moor Place' is a
pompon dahlia in a rich clerical
red'; 'Hamari Gold' is a multi-
petalled decorative dahlia in a
bright, warm golden orange, and
'Princess Marie José' is a single-
flowered dahlia in soft pink.
ht 60cm–1m/2–3ft
sp 45–60cm/18–24in

Soil and position
Fairly heavy, fertile soil and a
sunny position.

Eranthis hyemalis
WINTER ACONITE

Bright yellow, buttercup flowers
surrounded by green ruffs open
on short stems in late winter, at
the same time as the snowdrops,
advising us that we'll soon be
getting into our gardening boots
again. In summer the plants
disappear, to put out leaf again
the following winter. Over the
course of the years, provided
they are at home, they will
spread to form large clumps.
ht and sp 8–10cm/3–4in
Soil and situation
A well-drained, moist soil that
doesn't dry out in summer and a
sunny or semi-shaded position.

▶ Dahlia *'Bishop of Llandaff'* has
brilliant red flowers and black foliage.

Galtonia candicans, the fragrant, white-flowered form, is the one most usually grown but there is also a more unusual galtonia with pale green flowers, *G. viridiflora*. They flower in late summer. Mulch the plants for winter protection in all but the mildest areas.
ht 1m/3ft
sp 20cm/8in
Soil and position
Well-drained soil that remains slightly moist in summer and a sunny, fairly sheltered position.

Iris
IRIS
Broadly, irises divide into two types: bulbous (grown from bulbs, and usually quite small) and rhizomatous (grown from rhizomes, and including the larger irises as well as some dwarf ones). Many of the rhizomatous kind are bearded, with rough crests on the three large, dropping outer petals or 'falls' characteristic of all irises.

Bulbous irises include Spanish, English and Dutch. Dutch flower in white, yellow and blue in early summer, with the English (white, purple and blue), and Spanish (white, purple, blue and yellow), flowering later. Another bulbous type is the small and lovely winter-flowering *Iris reticulata* (with flowers in blue or purple).

Beardless, moisture-loving rhizomatous irises include the mid-summer-flowering *I. pseudacorus*, the yellow flag or water iris, a must for streams and pondsides, and *I. sibirica* or Siberian flag, with blue or purple early summer flowers.

Bearded rhizomatous irises come in all sizes, from dwarf to tall. Two good, fragrant ones are *I. pallida* 'Variegata' with lilac blue flowers and green and yellow striped leaves, and the lovely winter-flowering *Iris*

▶ Iris reticulata, *a bulbous iris.*

unguicularis, almost hiding its low-growing lavender, blue and lilac flowers among its leaves. Other favourites include 'Langport Smoke' in a clear, soft blue; 'Langport Song', with ruffled, lemon-yellow petals; 'Black Knight', dark purple; 'Bronze Cloud', copper and lavender blue, and 'Dante', golden bronze and raspberry red.
ht and sp 5–100cm/2–39in
Soil and position
Bulbous irises need well-drained soil and an open, sunny, sheltered position. Rhizomatous irises generally like warm, alkaline soil and a sunny, sheltered position, but the beardless, pondside ones like moist soil and semi-shade, and yellow flag will grow in water at the pond edge.
CAUTION: CAN CAUSE STOMACH UPSET IF EATEN.

Leucojum aestivum 'Gravetye'
SUMMER SNOWFLAKE OR LODDON LILY
Leucojum plants look like enlarged snowdrops. Small, flaring, bell-like flowers, in white, with green spots on the pointed tepal (a kind of petal) tips, hang prettily from the stem tops, just above the narrow, straplike leaves. *Leucojum aestivum* 'Gravetye' is a reliable variety which flowers in late spring. The lower-growing *L. vernum* flowers in early spring.
ht to 60cm/2ft (Leucojum aestivum)*; 20cm/8in* (L. vernum)
sp 10cm/4in
Soil and position
Moist soil and dappled shade.

Lilium
LILY
Lilies are a firm gardening favourite. They offer a huge choice, and the following are just a few favourites among lilies that

are undemanding and fairly easy to obtain. *Lilium candidum*, the madonna lily (white, very fragrant, midsummer flowering, and one of the few to need alkaline soil); *L. longiflorum*, the Easter lily (actually flowering in midsummer, very fragrant, lime-tolerant); *L. regale*, the regal lily (fragrant, white, with deep pink streaks on the outside, midsummer flowering); *L. mackliniae* (pink, unscented, midsummer flowering); *L. monadelphum* (fragrant, creamy yellow, purple-spotted inside, flowering early summer, tolerates lime); *L.* 'Enchantment' (rich orange, flowering early summer, not scented); *L.* 'Star Gazer' (beautiful reddish-pink flowers with darker spots; midsummer flowering).
ht to 1m/3ft or more; to 60cm/2ft (L. mackliniae)
sp 15–20cm/6–8in

◀ Nerine bowdenii, *nerine.*

ht 10–15cm/4–8in
sp 5cm/2in
Soil and position
Almost any reasonably well-drained soil in a sunny position.

Narcissus
DAFFODIL AND JONQUIL

There are far too many narcissi to begin to select – from short for rockeries and pots to tall for borders and from early to late flowerers. Among the smaller ones 'Tête à Tête' is a dwarf in cheerful yellow for early spring, 'Minnow' is a pale dwarf for mid-spring, *N. cyclamineus* is an early-flowering species with backward flaring perianths and long, narrow trumpets, and *N. cantabricus* is an enchanting white hooped petticoat daffodil with wide funnel-shaped trumpets and tiny pointed perianths. Late in the season *N. poeticus*, a tall species, produces fragrant white flowers with tiny orange cups instead of trumpets. The many hybrids include: 'Actaea' (white with orange centres); 'Carlton' (soft yellow); 'February Gold' (bright yellow); 'Ice Follies' (one of the best and most beautiful white varieties); 'King Alfred' (sturdy, with bright yellow flowers); 'Minnow' a dainty dwarf, with lemon yellow flowers); 'Pinza' (rich yellow with red cups); and 'Rainbow' (white and pink). Sturdy hybrids are useful for naturalizing in grass.
ht 20–50cm/8–20in, sp16cm/6in (hybrids and N. poeticus*);*
ht 15–20cm/6-8in,
sp 5–8cm/2–3in (the rest)
Soil and position
Ordinary garden soil and a sunny, light position.

Nerine bowdenii
NERINE

Nerines have wavy, loosely grouped lily-like flowers on tall, narrow stems, and strap-shaped, rather grass-like leaves; they flower from late summer and right through the autumn, making them even more appreciated. While most species are not suitable for growing outdoors in our climate *Nerine bowdenii*, with its light raspberry pink flowers, is hardy and robust. *N. b.* 'Mark Fenwick' (aka 'Fenwick's Variety') is a stronger and taller variety, with deeper pink flowers, and *N. b. f. alba* has white or palest pink flowers.
ht 50cm/20in
sp 8cm/3in
Soil and position
Well-drained soil in a sunny and sheltered position, for example by a house wall.

Tulipa
TULIP

You can buy mixed tulips in unspecified colours and they will flower cheerfully in later spring, but sometimes only a special tulip will do. Among the many stunning varieties are 'Angelique' (double, pale pink); 'Golden Apeldorn' (bright yellow with black base), 'Queen of Night' (very dark, almost black); 'Spring Green' (white flowers with green feathering); 'White Parrot', and 'Black Parrot' (with twisting, fringed petals in white/almost black). Finally the small, early flowering water-lily tulip *T. kaufmanniana* has wide-open, scented flowers in cream or yellow, sometimes with contrasting centres.
ht 30cm/12in ('Angelique');
60cm/24in ('Golden Apeldorn' and 'Queen of Night');
40cm/16in ('Spring Green');
55cm/22in ('White Parrot', and 'Black Parrot'); 20cm/8in
(T. kaufmanniana)
sp 8–15cm/3–6in
Soil and position
Well-drained soil in a sunny, fairly sheltered position.

Soil and situation
Unless otherwise stated lilies require well-drained neutral or acid soil enriched with compost or leaf mould and a position in sun or lightly dappled shade.

Muscari
GRAPE HYACINTH

Grape hyacinths produce blue flowers arranged like miniature grapes on upright stems in spring, surrounded by a mass of somewhat untidy arching, grassy leaves. Unnamed varieties are generally available but it's worth looking out for *Muscari neglectum* (syn. *M. racemosum*), which has white-rimmed flowers in very deep blue, and *M. aucheri*, whose pale blue, almost drumhead flowers are again white rimmed and whose leaves are a pleasant greyish green.

PERENNIALS

Perennials form the mainstay of most garden planting, lasting from year to year and normally flowering annually. We have included in this section not only herbaceous perennials that die back over winter and grow up again in spring, but also some of the smaller shrubs. The plants listed here include some that flower in winter and autumn as well as spring and summer.

Alchemilla mollis
LADY'S MANTLE

This is a 'must-have' for almost any type of garden, at home in a formal or informal setting. Bundles of tiny, greenish yellow flowers weigh down the light stems for the whole summer and the downy, lobed leaves catch drops of rain or dew at the centre. The plant lolls gracefully at the front of a border, forms large clumps, and self-seeds. Grows prettily in gravel or between the paving stones too.

ht 60cm/2ft
sp 75cm/30in
Soil and position
Prefers a fairly moist, rich soil but tolerates dry, fairly poor soils too. Thrives equally well in sun or semi-shade.
SLUGS AND SNAILS CAN ATTACK YOUNG LEAVES.

Anemone × hybrida
(syn. *A. japonica*)
JAPANESE ANEMONE

A tall and lovely plant for later summer, with flowers of white or shades of moody pink on upright, branching stems. The simple flowers, wide open and with a central boss of orange-yellow stamens are mainly single, as in the white 'Honorine Jobert', but 'Whirlwind' (white) and 'Queen Charlotte' (pink) are semi-double. The deeply toothed leaves cluster beautifully round the stem axils.

ht 1.2m/4ft
sp 60cm/2ft
Soil and position
Needs moist but well-drained, rich soil in sun or semi-shade.

Aquilegia
AQUILEGIA

Aquilegia, also known as columbine, granny's bonnets and old maid's bonnets, is a well-loved, old-fashioned garden plant and there are many hybrids, named and unnamed. Its flower bonnets with their distinctive spurs nod down from graceful stems which rise up from a mass of lobed leaves, often a greyish green. Flowering in early summer, this is a pretty plant for a cottage garden or meadow garden. Not long-lived, but generally self-seeding it will often colonize an area when it feels at home.

Types to choose include *A. vulgaris* hybrids, including the neatly frilled 'Nora Barlow'; *A.* Mrs Scott Elliott Hybrids, often bi-coloured with very long spurs; *A. longissima*, pale yellow flowers with very long spurs; *A. flabellata*, soft blue.

ht 90cm/3ft
sp 60cm/2ft
Soil and position
Likes well-drained soil and cool conditions.

Campanula persicifolia
BELLFLOWER/CAMPANULA

There are many garden campanulas, including low-growing alpine varieties, most having flaring tube- or bell-shaped flowers in shades of blue, with white, some cream, and the occasional pink. *Campanula persicifolia* is tall and spiry, with slender stems sporting delicate-looking, harebell-like flowers of sky blue. *C. p. alba* is a similar white-flowered version. Slightly more uncommon, the smaller

C. alliariifolia has stems of downward-facing, narrow, white flowers and *C.* 'Elizabeth' has extremely narrow, pink-flushed flowers, offset by deep-toothed foliage. All flower from mid- to late summer, especially if the stems are cut after flowering. Beware of tiny slugs and snails, which can ravage the flowers.

ht 90cm/3ft (C. persicifolia);
45cm/18in (C. alliariifolia); to 40cm/16in (C. 'Elizabeth')
sp 30cm/12in (C. persicifolia);
45cm/18in (C. alliariifolia); to 40cm/16in (C. 'Elizabeth')
Soil and position
Like moist but well-drained soil and partial shade.

Crambe cordifolia
COLEWORT

Tall, spreading and airy, this plant from the cabbage family has

▲ Anemone × hybrida *(syn. A. japonica) Japanese anemone.*

many-branching stems and a froth of tiny white flowers against enormous veined and crinkled leaves. The flowers are fragrant, and attractive to bees. *Crambe maritima* or sea kale is similar but low-growing and with thick, bluish leaves; it grows well in maritime conditions. Both plants flower in early summer. The stems of sea kale can be blanched in winter for spring eating.

ht 1.8m/6ft (C. cordifolia);
75cm/30in (C. maritima)
sp 1.8m/6ft (C. cordifolia);
60cm/2ft (C. maritima)
Soil and position
Need a sunny position, sheltered from wind, in well-drained, alkaline soil.

Dicentra spectabilis
BLEEDING HEART

In late spring and early summer the fleshy, dark pink stems of graceful *Dicentra spectabilis* (called by country people 'ladies in the bath') are bowed with pink lockets hanging along their length. In the form *Dicentra spectabilis* 'Alba' the flowers are white and the stems green and more wiry. The plants form feathery-leaved clumps. *Dicentra formosa* is a similar but much lower growing plant.

ht 75cm/30in (Dicentra spectabilis); to 45cm/18in (Dicentra formosa)
sp 45cm/18in (Dicentra spectabilis); to 45cm/18in (Dicentra formosa)
Soil and position
Moist but well-drained, compost-rich soil in a sheltered, shady spot. Likes alkaline conditions.

Echinops
GLOBE THISTLE

Strong and sturdy, these plants have round drumheads of blue, thistle-like flowers and spiny, down-backed, grey-green leaves. The flowers, produced towards the end of the summer, are very attractive to bees, and dry well for dried flower arrangements. *E. bannaticus* 'Blue Globe' and the slightly more compact *E. ritro* 'Veitch's Blue' both have particularly well-coloured flowers.

ht to 1m/3ft
sp 45–60cm/18–24in
Soil and position
Although at their best in full sun and poor, fairly dry, well-drained soil, globe thistles will grow in almost any position.

Epimedium
BARRENWORT

Sometimes known as bishop's mitre or bishop's hat from the shape of their leaves, these are excellent ground-cover plants, especially for growing under trees and shrubs. There are many types available, and although they are grown mainly for their leaves many have attractive small flowers in yellow, orange, red or pink. Choice varieties include *E. × rubrum*, with crimson flowers and red and reddish brown leaves that are particularly striking in winter; *E. × versicolor* 'Cupreum', which is very tolerant and has

◀ *Eryngium, sea holly.*

coppery leaves and pink flowers; and *E. × v.* 'Sulphureum', with coppery leaves and yellow flowers. Check other species when you buy, as some are fussy and some die down in winter.

ht to 30cm/12in
sp indefinite
Soil and position
Woodland conditions with semi-shade to full shade, and moist, humus-rich soil.

Eryngium
SEA HOLLY

The overall effect of these architectural plants, with their holly-like leaves and cone-shaped flowers surrounded by arresting, spiny bracts, is of spiky shapes and grey-blue or metallic blue colouring. *Eryngium × oliverianum* is a good long-lived variety with silvery blue colouring that ages to purple-blue, while *E. × tripartitum*, also long-lived, is slightly taller, lighter in form, and more dainty, with violet-blue colouring. All flower until the autumn and are good for cutting and drying.

ht 60cm–1m/2–3ft
sp50–60cm/20–24in
Soil and position
Needs a sunny position and very well-drained soil that does not get waterlogged during the winter months.

Euphorbia
SPURGE, MILKWEED

Great favourites with knowledgeable gardeners, spurges provide a wide choice of bushy plants, generally evergreen, with strong, sappy stems, often a leaning habit, and flowers of yellowish green.
E. nicaeensis★ has domes of lime-yellow, green-bracted flowers in spring and blue-green, curling leaves growing all the way down the strong stems. *E. characias*★ is

tall and erect with densely flowered stems. Its flowers have purple nectar glands, though the sub-species known as *E.c. wulfenii* has greenish yellow flowers. The much smaller *E. polychroma* is very lime-yellow, starry flowering and mound forming. Other spurges to consider are *E. amygdaloides*★★, *E. cyparissias*★, *E. myrsinites*★, *E. griffithii* 'Dixter'★★ and *E. g.* 'Fireglow'★★.

ht 80cm/32in; sp 45cm/18in (E. nicaeensis)
ht and sp 1.2m/4ft (E. characias)
ht 40cm/16in; sp 60cm/2ft (E. polychroma)
ht 75cm/30in; sp 30cm/12in (E. amygdaloides)
ht 20–40cm/8–16in; sp indefinite (E. cyparissias)
ht 10cm/4in; sp to 30cm/12in (E. myrsinites)
ht 75cm/30in; sp 90cm/3ft (E. griffithii)
Soil and position
Those marked ★ like a sunny spot in well-drained soil; those marked ★★ need light, dappled shade and a moist soil with plenty of humus. *E. polychroma* adapts to sun or partial shade.

CAUTION: THE MILKY WHITE LIQUID IN THE STEMS IS POISONOUS IF INGESTED AND CAUSTIC TO THE TOUCH.

Geranium
CRANESBILL, GERANIUM

You can become addicted to geraniums and their modest charms. These are hardy, and, given conditions they like, very long-lasting plants, with flowers in shades of pale pink to magenta, white, and light sky blue. They have lobed or deeply cut leaves and simple, wide-open flowers, often delicately veined or deeply stained at the centre, and they vary from small and compact to large clump-forming. Among the best are the very reliable G. 'Johnson's Blue', with warm blue flowers; G. *sanguineum* 'Album' (white), G. *s.* 'Shepherd's Warning' (deep pink), and G. *s.* var. *striatum* (pale pink, delicately marked with deeper pink). G. *renardii*, which flourishes in poor soil, has velvety leaves and dark-veined pale lavender flowers. The meadow cranesbill, G. *pratense*, is blue, with white varieties, and

flourishes in meadow-type conditions with rich, moist soil. The large G. *maderense*, (evergreen leaves, red stems, light magenta flowers) is short-lived in gardens but easily grown annually from seed.

ht to 45cm/18in, sp to 75cm/30in (G. 'Johnson's Blue')
ht 30cm/12in, sp 40cm/16in (G. sanguineum 'Album')
ht and sp 15cm/6in (G. s. 'Shepherd's Warning')
ht and sp 10cm/4in (G. s. var. striatum)
ht and sp 30cm/12in (G. renardii)
ht to 90cm/3ft sp 60cm/24ft (G. pratense)
ht and sp to 1.5m/5ft (G. maderense)
Soil and position
Unless stated above geraniums are happy in ordinary, well-drained garden soil, in sun or partial shade. The smallest species need very good drainage, with added grit or sharp sand.

Helleborus argutifolius
(syn. *H. corsicus*)
CORSICAN HELLEBORE

This large, shrubby-looking hellebore has bunches of small,

pale creamy green flowers for a long period from late winter and interesting, tooth-edged, leathery leaves throughout the year. The shorter *Helleborus foetidus* is very similar, also tough and shrubby looking, but with lime-green flowers, rimmed with crimson and lasting well into spring.

Shorter hellebores, best grown in groups, are the pure white *Helleborus niger* or Christmas rose and *Helleborus orientalis*, the lenten rose. Both have large and tender-looking, cup-like flowers, the first in late winter, the second in early spring. 'Potter's Wheel' is a good variety of the Christmas rose, generous with its pure white flowers. Lenten roses have plum coloured flowers and there are many subtly shaded hybrids, named and unnamed.

ht 90cm/3ft, sp to 1.2m/4ft (Helleborus argutifolius)
ht 60cm/24in, sp 45cm/18in (Helleborus foetidus)
ht and sp 30cm/12in (Helleborus niger)
ht and sp 45cm/18in (Helleborus orientalis)
Soil and position
Fertile, well-drained but moist, limy soil; shade or partial shade.
CAUTION: THE PLANTS ARE POISONOUS IF EATEN AND THE SAP CAN CAUSE IRRITATION.

Hemerocallis
DAY LILY

Members of the lily family, day lilies have sword-shaped leaves and twisting stems. They bear their flowers for only a day, but continue to produce new flowers during the whole of the summer. Many varieties have now been bred and there is a wide choice of colours and flower shapes, from spidery to double and triangular. The plants form large clumps. Among those

to choose are 'Berlin Red' and 'Red Precious' (red), 'Cartwheels' (orange), 'Lemon Bells', and Marion Vaughn', (shades of yellow), and 'Pink Damask' (pink). Shorter, so-called dwarf varieties such as 'Golden Chimes' and 'Stella de Oro' (yellow) are also available.

ht to 1.3m/4ft
sp to 90cm/3ft
Soil and position
A sunny position in fertile, moist, rather heavy but well-drained soil. Will also tolerate partial shade.

Heuchera
HEUCHERA OR CORAL FLOWER

A member of the saxifrage family, heuchera can be grown as ground cover in light shade, or in clumps in borders, where the flowers will attract bees. The plants make mounds of foliage out of which spring panicles of tiny flowers on tall stems. Most of the named varieties are red or coral pink but the species H. *cylindrica* offers green-flowered varieties such as 'Greenfinch', which can be used to much more subtle effect. Good red varieties include 'Red Spangles' and 'Coral Cloud'. If you want to use heuchera as a foliage plant try 'Palace Purple' (chocolate), 'Pewter Moon' (grey) or 'Snow Storm' (flecked white).

ht to 90cm/3ft, sp 60cm/2ft ('Greenfinch')
ht 50cm/20in, sp 25cm/10in ('Red Spangles')
ht 75cm/30in, sp 30cm/12in ('Coral Cloud')
ht and sp to 60cm/2ft ('Palace Purple')
ht to 40cm/16in, sp 30cm/12in ('Pewter Moon')
ht and sp 30cm/12in ('Snow Storm')
Soil and position
Moist but well-drained, preferably neutral soil in partial to full shade.

◀ Geranium, *cranesbill or geranium.*

Kniphofia
RED HOT POKER

Red hot poker is certainly a striking plant, in height, form and colour, and it can be just what's needed to make bright points of colour or as a foil to softer plants. Torches of red or orange flowers rise erect from the bundles of strap-like leaves in a show-stopping way in summer, with exact flowering times depending on the cultivar. Among the tall and reds you might choose the brilliant *K.* 'Atlanta' (red and yellow, flowering early summer), or the massive *K.* 'Prince Igor' (pure, brilliant red for the end of the summer). *K. caulescens* is a very hardy red hot poker with more muted colours (dull purple red topping light yellow), flowering from late summer into the autumn; the lower growing *K.* 'Bees Sunset' has warm light orange flowers throughout the summer, and for a yellow poker of modest height there is *K.* 'Sunningdale Yellow', which flowers from mid- to late summer.
ht 1.2m/4ft, sp 75cm/30in
('Atlanta')
ht 1.8m/6ft sp 90cm/3ft
('Prince Igor')
ht to 1.2m/4ft, sp 60cm/2ft
(K. caulescens)
ht 90cm/3ft, sp 60cm/2ft
('Bees Sunset')
ht 90cm/3ft, sp 45cm/18in
('Sunningdale Yellow') '
Soil and position
Fertile, sandy or well-drained soil in a sunny position. Tolerates light shade.

Lamium maculatum
LAMIUM OR DEAD NETTLE

Lamium is a ground-cover plant for shaded places, grown mainly for its tooth-edged white- and silver- mottled leaves. *Lamium maculatum* f. *album* has pure white flowers throughout the spring and early summer, as well as white-patterned leaves; *L. m.* 'Roseum' is its pink-flowered partner. *L. m.* 'White Nancy' has green-edged, silver leaves and white flowers, and *L. m.* 'Aureum' has yellow and white leaves, although (unusually for plants with golden variegation) like the rest, it must have semi-shade. The plants spread quickly and are hardy, keeping their leaves throughout the winter as long as it's not too wet.
ht 23–30cm/9–12in
sp to 60cm/2ft
Soil and position
Thrives in shade and semi-shade in ordinary soil. *L. m.* 'Aureum' needs more moisture and a more fertile soil than the others.

Lavandula
LAVENDER

Lavender (really a shrub) needs no introduction as a well-loved garden and herb garden plant for warm and well-drained sites. The flowers can be dried and used in pot pourri and for scenting linen. The bushy plants, with their grey-green leaves, look good even when not covered in the fragrant flower spikes. *Lavandula angustifolia* is the old English lavender, also know as *L. officinalis* or *L. spica*. The variety 'Hidcote' is a true deep lavender blue; the more compact 'Munstead' is purple blue. 'Hidcote Pink' is (as its name suggests) a pink-flowered form, while 'Nana Alba' is small and neat and white-flowering. A less hardy and more unusual lavender is French lavender, *L. stoechas*, with flaring purple bracts above the flowers.
ht 60cm/2ft, sp 75cm/30in
('Hidcote' and 'Hidcote Pink')
ht 45cm/18in, sp 60cm/2ft
('Munstead')
ht and sp 30cm/12in
('Nana Alba')
ht and sp 60cm/2ft (L. stoechas)

Soil and position
Very well-drained soil, and a position in full sun.

Papaver orientale
ORIENTAL POPPY

Gardens need poppies. *Papaver orientale* is the brilliant orange-red poppy commonly seen in established gardens, but there are many hybrids, known by their own names, giving a wide choice of colour and patterning. 'Black and White' is a luscious double creamy white poppy with black stamens; 'Bonfire Red' speaks for itself; 'Cedric Morris' has full-blown petals in soft pink, with black blotches at the centre; 'Beauty of Livermore' is a clear poppy red, and 'Mrs Perry' is black-blotched salmon pink.
(See also *Papaver*, page 76)
ht to 90cm/3ft
sp 60–90cm/2–3ft
Soil and position
Fertile soil, including heavy soil

▲ Kniphofia, *red hot poker.*

as long as it is well-drained, and a sunny position.

Penstemon cultivars
PENSTEMON

With their profusion of foxglove bells and their tall but bushy growth these are lovely, though not very hardy or long-lived border plants, which flower well into the autumn. In recent years more and more hybrids have been developed to widen the range of colours and improve hardiness. Colours vary from strong to pastel, mainly pinks, magenta and purples, but also blue and white. Give frost protection where winters are cold, and protect from slugs and snails, which are partial to this dish. All the following are hardy: 'Alice Hindley' (lilac blue), 'Apple Blossom' (apple blossom pink), 'Blackbird' (deep purple),

'Garnet' (garnet red), 'Hidcote Pink' (pale pink), 'Mother of Pearl' (pearly lilac and pink), 'White Bedder' (white).
ht and sp 10–60cm/4–24in
Soil and position
Penstemons need fertile soil with good drainage, especially during winter, and a warm, sheltered position in sun or partial shade.

Perovskia atriplicifolia
PEROVSKIA

More people should grow this tolerant, shrubby plant for its tiny lilac blue flowers and grey-green, sage-scented leaves on wiry stems. The flowers are produced towards the end of the summer but, with its mass of tall and upward-branching greyish stems and narrow, tooth-edged leaves, the plant looks good all summer. *P.* 'Blue Spire' is very generous with its deep violet-

blue flowers. *P.* 'Hybrida' has lavender-blue flowers and is a little less tall.
ht 90cm–1.5m/3–5ft
sp to 90cm/3ft
Soil and position
Needs a sunny position in freely draining soil but will grow in poor, dry or chalky soil. May not survive winter in cold, damp conditions, but may revive if cut back in spring.

Phlox paniculata
GARDEN PHLOX

With their evocative, slightly woody scent and heads of simple, open flowers, these are good, long-lived herbaceous border plants. They flower in full summer, mostly in the pink, white and dusky purple colour range, and often with a contrasting eye. Good specimens include 'Alba Grandiflora'

▶ *Penstemon* cultivars, penstemon.

(white), 'Amethyst' (violet), 'Blue Ice' (blue-tinged white with contrasting eye), 'Eva Callum' (deep pink with contrasting eye), 'Eventide' (lavender blue), 'Prince of Orange' (orange-red), 'Prospero' (pale lilac, white edged), and 'White Admiral' (pure white). Plants may need staking in windy spots and frequent watering in dry weather.
ht 80cm–1.2m/32in–4ft
sp 60–90cm/2–3ft
Soil and position
Fertile, heavy, moist but well-drained soil and a position in sun or partial shade.

Potentilla
POTENTILLA

There is a huge range of potentillas for the garden. They are in fact shrubs, but many make nice, well-rounded little bushes, small enough to blend well with perennials and border plants. They have attractive small leaves, sometimes deeply cut or silvery, and are usually covered with small and delicate buttercup-like flowers from early summer until late autumn.

Flowers are in white and all shades of yellow, orange, red or pink. Among the many small garden hybrids are *Potentilla* 'Gibson's Scarlet' (blood-red flowers with dark centres), 'William Rollinson' (semi-double, flowers in red flecked with yellow) and *P. nepalensis* 'Miss Willmott' (raspberry pink with carmine markings). *P. recta* (pale lemon-yellow) and *P. fruticosa* 'Abbotswood' (delicate white flowers) are a little larger.
ht 30–45cm/12–18in, sp 60cm/ 2ft ('Gibson's Scarlet', 'William Rollinson', 'Miss Willmott')

◀ *Lamium maculatum,* Lamium or dead nettle.

ht 60cm/2ft, sp 45cm/18in (P. recta)
ht 75cm/30in, sp 1.2m/4ft (P. fruticosa 'Abbotswood')
Soil and position
Must have very well-drained soil, which need not be too fertile. Flower best in full sun.

Pulmonaria
PULMONARIA OR LUNGWORT

Also known as soldiers and sailors, this is a lovely low-growing plant for early spring, one of the first to flower, and growing bigger and better as the season continues. When the flowers are over the white-blotched leaves come to the fore, and remain decoratively in the garden all summer and autumn. The flowers are a beautiful blue, or in some varieties varicoloured pink and blue. Choice white varieties are also available, and a few are pink or red. Good blue varieties include *Pulmonaria* 'Mawson's Blue' (deep blue), *P. officinalis* 'Royal Blue' and *P. o.* 'Blue Mist'. *P. o.* 'Sissinghurst White' is the white to go for.

ht and sp 30cm/12in
Soil and position
Moist, fertile soil and a position in partial shade. Lungwort grows well beneath deciduous trees and shrubs.

Sedum spectabile
ICE PLANT

There is something cactus-like about this plant, with its fleshy, grey-green stems and leaves, and its densely packed flat flower heads of starry pink flowers

attracting butterflies in late summer. The plant has a rounded, compact shape and dry flower heads are an attraction throughout the winter. *Sedum spectabile* 'Autumn Joy' and *S. s.* 'Brilliant' are good varieties.

ht and sp 45cm/18in
Soil and position
Grows best in well-drained slightly alkaline soil, in full sun.

Stachys byzantina
LAMB'S EARS OR LAMB'S TONGUE

Soft, silver-grey and felted leaves are the main feature of this plant for dry places, although in summer it also has taller spikes of small purplish pink flowers set in whorls among tiny grey leaves and rising above the lamb's ear leaves. It also spreads well and is evergreen – or evergrey – except

▶ Pulmonaria, *pulmonaria or lungwort,* 'Mawson's Blue' *cultivar.*

that a damp winter can end its life.

ht to 45cm/18in
sp 60cm/2ft
Soil and position
Must have very well-drained soil (though will tolerate poor soil), and an open, fairly sunny position.

Verbascum
VERBASCUM OR MULLEIN

An elegant, tall, spiry plant with grey, felted leaves, verbascum is sometimes short-lived but is easily grown from seed. The flower spike ascends from a rosette of leaves in summer and some varieties are very tall. *Verbascum bombyciferum* with its immense height and sulphur-yellow flowers is an accent plant and a half. Many named garden varieties are available for those who want something a little less lofty or more subtly coloured. *V.* 'Cotswold Beauty' has purple-centred yellow flowers; the flowers of 'Gainsborough' are chalky yellow, and 'Pink Domino' has rosy or purple pink

flowers. *V. phoeniceum* (purple mullein) hybrids give pink, white and purple flowers.

ht 1.2m/4ft; to 1.6m/6ft (Verbascum bombyciferum)
sp 30–60cm/1–2ft
Soil and position
Alkaline, well-drained to dry soil, including poor soils. Does best in sun.

Verbena bonariensis
VERBENA

Tall, wiry, branching stems produce many small heads of bright purple flowers throughout the summer and early autumn at varying heights. The stems are spruce green and pleasantly rough. Sometimes grown as an annual bedding plant, verbena survives the winter if protected from frost.

ht to 1.2m/4ft
sp 45cm/18in
Soil and position
Well-drained soil and full sun.

◀ Sedum specatabile, *ice plant.*

TREES AND SPECIMEN SHRUBS

Trees and shrubs give shape and form to the garden and can act as strong focal points. They need to be chosen and positioned with care as they make a permanent feature that can take up a lot of room, and make areas of shade, but they compensate by adding height and substance and helping to bring structure to the plot. The plants selected here are all suitable for smaller gardens and many have something of interest to offer for more than one season.

Acer
MAPLE

There are several ornamental maples whose height keeps to within ordinary garden limits, and they usually have bark appeal as well as leaf appeal and autumn colour. *Acer* 'Silver Vein' is a snake-bark maple with silver striping on its trunk and broad, flat, three-lobed leaves which turn a glorious yellow in the autumn. An advantage is that it can be grown as a single- or multi-stemmed tree. *Acer henryi* is a smallish, shapely maple which colours bright orange-red in autumn and *Acer rufinerve* (another snake-bark maple) is a taller but less spreading maple with green and white striped bark, and red and orange leaves in autumn.
ht and sp 5–10m/16–32ft
Soil and position
Fertile, well-drained (but not dry) soil, preferably in a light position.

Amelanchier lamarckii
AMELANCHIER
OR SNOWY MESPILUS

Bronze unfolding leaves almost disappear as small white starry flowers smother the branches of the plant in spring. Amelanchier

becomes less interesting as the flowers die and leaves turn green, but in later summer coral pink fruits develop and then the leaves turn bright red. If the birds leave the fruits to ripen they eventually turn black.

▲ Acer palmatum, 'Dissectum Atropurpureum', Japanese maple.

Can be grown as a single or multi-stemmed plant.
ht 3m/10ft
sp to 3m/10ft

Soil and position
Moist, preferably neutral or acid soil in a light position.

Berberis sieboldii
BERBERIS OR BARBERRY

A spiny shrub with shiny reddish stems and clusters of small yellow flowers in late spring. In autumn these develop into red shining berries and the pointed leaves turn a magnificent vivid red in a display that lasts over a long period. The plant can be grown in a wide range of soils.
ht and sp 90–120cm/3–4ft
Soil and position
Likes soils from sandy to almost boggy and a position in full sun.
CAUTION: TAKE CARE WHEN HANDLING BARBERRY BECAUSE OF ITS SPINES. ALL PARTS OF THE PLANT CAN CAUSE STOMACH UPSETS IF EATEN.

Buddleia davidii
BUDDLEJA
OR BUTTERFLY BUSH

Most people know buddleia, with its arching branches of honey-scented flowers that attract butterflies to the garden in late summer. Growing in densely covered plumes, the flowers are normally in shades of purple, from light soft bluish purple to deepest royal purple, though they also come in white. *Buddleja davidii* 'Black Knight' has the darkest flowers, 'Empire Blue' has lavender blue flowers, 'Harlequin' is cerise and has cream-margined leaves, and 'White Profusion' has very long tails of white flowers. The species *B. alternifolia*, with more delicate, clustered flowers and willow-like leaves, is a more unusual alternative that flowers earlier in the year.
ht to 3m/10ft
sp to 4.5m/15ft
Soil and position
Ordinary, well-drained garden soil in full sun.

8 9

◀ Buddleja davidii *'Black Knight'*, buddleia or butterfly bush.

Ceanothus 'Gloire de Versailles'
CEANOTHUS OR CALIFORNIA LILAC

From ground-level upward, pale blue powderpuffs of flowers enliven this hardy California lilac all summer. Ceanothus makes a lovely plant for a warm, sheltered spot and grows well against a wall; many forms are to be found. 'Gloire de Versailles' is deciduous but in the late-spring-flowering 'Cascade' the little leaves are evergreen and the flowers a brighter blue.
ht and sp 1.5m/5ft or more ('Gloire de Versailles'); up to 3.6m/12ft ('Cascade')
Soil and position
These shrubs need good drainage and like poor, sandy soil. They must have warmth, and shelter from cold winds.

Cornus kousa var. chinensis
KOUSA DOGWOOD

This is a neat, upright shrub or small tree with minute green flowers surrounded by showy white bracts. In hot summers the flowers sometimes develop strawberry-like fruits and the tapered oval leaves are a bright crimson red in autumn.
ht to 7m/23ft
sp 4.5m/15ft
Soil and position
Almost any soil, as long as well-drained, and a position in sun or partial shade.

Cornus officinalis
DOGWOOD

This very hardy multi-stemmed dogwood is grown for its grey, brown and orange winter bark and purple-red autumn leaves. Tolerant of most soils, it is very vigorous. Other dogwoods with colourful stems include *C. stolonifera* (dark red), *C. stolonifera* 'Flaviramea' (yellow-green), and *C. alba* (red). All look good growing near water, or where the winter light can filter through the stems.
ht and sp 3m/10ft (C. alba);
ht and sp to 4.5m/15ft (C. officinalis); ht 1.8m/6ft, sp 3.6m/12ft (C. stolonifera)
Soil and position
Ordinary garden soil in an open, sunny position.

Cotinus
SMOKE BUSH

The smoke bush has leaves that colour brightly in autumn and flowers that create the impression of plumes of smoke in summer. *Cotinus* 'Grace' has red and orange leaves in autumn; *Cotinus coggygria* 'Royal Purple' has smoky pink plumes of flowers and purple foliage which provides a foil for many garden flowers and which colours bright red in autumn.
ht and sp 5m/16ft
Soil and position
Ordinary garden soil and a sunny position to bring out the best foliage colour.

Cotoneaster
COTONEASTER

Cotoneasters are a family of very obliging shrubs which produce a wealth of red berries to attract the birds in autumn and generally keep their leaves throughout the winter. The leaves are dark green and often colour up to red during the winter. In late spring plants bear a mass of small white flowers. The handsome, tree-like *Cotoneaster* 'Cornubia' has broad, semi-evergreen leaves and bright bunches of clear red fruits which weigh down the stems in autumn and often last all winter. *C.* 'Exburiensis' has yellow fruits.
ht and sp 6m/20ft ('Cornubia'); 4.5m/15ft ('Exburiensis')
Soil and position
Ordinary well-drained, or even dry, soil in sun or partial shade.

Elaeagnus pungens
ELAEAGNUS

This is a strong evergreen shrub with glossy green leaves, making it particularly useful in winter. In the variety 'Maculata' the leaves are gold outlined with deep green, and 'Dicksonii' has yellow-edged leaves. Elaeagnus has small but extremely fragrant cream-coloured tubular flowers in autumn.
ht and sp to 4m/13ft or more but can be kept trimmed
Soil and position
Puts up with most soils and situations, including by the sea.

Eucalyptus gunnii
EUCALYPTUS OR CIDER GUM

This is a fast-growing Tasmanian tree that flourishes in European climates. The rounded young leaves, like the peeling bark, are a silvery grey, and the plant may produce more than one trunk. The leaves are evergreen and the young leaves are the prettiest, so the stems are best cut back each year in early spring to encourage new growth. The tree produces creamy white flowers in late summer to early autumn.
ht 14m/46ft
sp 4.5m/15ft or more

*Can be grown as a shrub trimmed to
ht 1.8m/6ft, sp 1.2m/4ft*
Soil and position
Fertile, slightly acid, moist soil
and a sunny position with shelter
from cold winds.

Fothergilla major
FOTHERGILLA

Scented, cream-coloured fuzzy
flowers in spring before the
leaves appear and radiant yellow
or yellow and scarlet leaves in
autumn make this a shrub for
two seasons. It spreads broadly
and is fairly low-growing.
Fothergilla gardenii is similar but
smaller and more compact and
with crimson autumn leaves.
*ht to 2.5m/8ft, sp to 1.8m/6ft
(Fothergilla major); ht 90cm/3ft,
sp to 1.2m/4ft (F. gardenii)*
Soil and position
Needs light, acid soil and will
flourish in any position from full
sun to semi-shade.

Genista aetnensis
MOUNT ETNA BROOM

Graceful and arching, brooms
make fountains of golden flowers
in the summer months. Mount
Etna broom makes a rounded
small tree, the stems completely
hidden by flowers in full
summer. *G. cineria* is a lower-
growing multi-stemmed shrub,
billowing with sweetly scented
flowers in early summer.
*ht to 6m/20ft, sp to 5.5m/18ft
(Genista aetnensis); ht to 3m/10ft,
sp to 2.5m/8ft (G. cineria)*
Soil and position
Light, well-drained soil,
including poor soil, and a warm,
sunny position.

Hamamelis mollis
HAMAMELIS OR CHINESE
WITCH HAZEL

Witch hazel is a must for anyone
who wants winter fragrance. The
wispy yellow flowers on the bare
twigs actually benefit from cold,
which prolongs the flowering

▶ *Cotinus*, smoke bush, requires a
sunny position for best colour.

period; the rounded leaves turn a
soft warm yellow in autumn.
H. × intermedia 'Pallida' (syn *H. m.*
'Pallida') has red-centred, pale
yellow flowers. Plant hamamelis
near the house or the front path,
so that you can sniff it when you
walk by.
ht and sp to 2.5m/8ft
Soil and position
Needs a fairly rich, moist soil
that is neutral to acid and a
sheltered spot in full sun or
semi-shade.

Hebe
HEBE

Hebes are staunch plants,
keeping their small, leathery
leaves all year and flowering for a
long period, as well as forming
neat, compact bushes that
generally grow well in
containers. In some varieties the
leaves are variegated, while the
numerous small flowers are
usually in shades of bluish
purple, with some pink- or
white-flowering varieties.
H. 'Autumn Glory' has flowers
in a warm purple blue, while
H. 'Midsummer Beauty' has lilac
coloured flowers fading to
white, and both flower from
mid-summer until late autumn.
H. speciosa 'Sapphire' is covered
in flowers of a warm, soft blue.
*ht to 1.5m/5ft
sp 1.2–1.5m/4–5ft*
Soil and position
Almost any soil, including chalk,
as long as it's well-drained, and a
sunny position. Hebes dislike real
cold, but withstand salt-laden
winds well.

Kolkwitzia amabilis
BEAUTY BUSH

A mass of delicate silvery pink
flowers gives rise to the name
beauty bush. The shrub can be
difficult to get started, but it

rewards persistence, producing its
lightly-scented foxglove-like
flowers on arching branches in
late spring and early summer.
*ht to 3.6m/12ft
sp to 3m/10ft
Can be pruned to keep it smaller.*
Soil and position
Ordinary, well-drained soil in a
sunny position. Flowers best in a
soil that is not too rich.

Lonicera periclymenum
HONEYSUCKLE

Honeysuckle climbs by twining
and can be grown on trellis or
fencing or over a large shrub.
A lovely plant for a scented
arbour or to grow against the
house wall, round the door, or
over a garden shed. All varieties

of *Lonicera periclymenum* have the
heady honeysuckle scent.
Here are some excellent choices:
L. p. 'Belgica' (purplish red and
yellowish cream) flowers in late
spring and early summer;
L. p. 'Graham Thomas' (white,
becoming yellow) flowers
through from midsummer until
the autumn; and *L. p.* 'Serotina'
(creamy white inside, purple-red
outside) flowers from mid-
summer until late autumn.
*ht and sp 3.6–6m/12–20ft
Can be trimmed to suit the space.*
Soil and situation
Ordinary, well-drained soil with
added compost or manure.
Flourishes in partial shade but
will do well in sun if the roots
are shaded.

◀ Lonicera periclymenum, *honeysuckle.*

Malus
CRAB APPLE

Crab apple trees are grown for their fragrant spring apple blossom and small and ornamental apple-like fruits that generally last from autumn and into the next spring. Good and fairly compact specimens include *Malus* 'Crittenden', profusely covered in apple-blossom pink flowers followed by small bunches of bright red berries; *M.* 'Golden Hornet', with white flowers and warm yellow crab apples, and *Malus × arnoldiana*, which has pink flowers opening from pinky red buds and fading to white, followed by red-flushed yellow fruits.
ht 4.5–5.5m/15–18ft
sp to 6m/20ft
Soil and position
Ordinary to rich garden soil which is well-drained, in sun or partial shade.

Pieris japonica
PIERIS

This is a large and spreading evergreen shrub with cascades of little vase-shaped, waxy flowers in spring and copper red new leaves. The variety 'Debutante' is slow-growing and very hardy, and in mid-spring its leaves are almost hidden by a mass of creamy white flowers. Unlike most other forms of pieris this one is a dwarf, making it ideal for smaller gardens, roof gardens or patios.
ht and sp to 3m/10ft
Soil and position
Must have lime-free, well-drained soil; flowers best in full sun. Provide shelter from cold winds to prevent frost damage.

Potentilla
POTENTILLA

Potentillas come in all sizes and the small ones can be thought of as belonging with perennials. As a larger shrub, *Potentilla fruticosa* var. *arbuscula* (syn. *P. arbuscula*) comes in many varieties, with flower colours in all shades of yellow and orange, as well as white, pink and red. The buttercup-like flowers occur over a very long period from late spring onwards. All have pretty leaves, some finely dissected.
ht 90cm–1.5m/3–5ft
sp to 1.5m/5ft
Soil and position
Light, or even poor soil, as long as it is well-drained; a light, sunny position is required for best flowering.
(See also page 87)

Prunus
PRUNUS OR
FLOWERING CHERRY

The term 'prunus' covers a huge range of flowering cherries, plums and almond trees, many grown only for their clouds of spring flowers and not bearing fruit. Among these one of the loveliest is *Prunus* 'Shirotae', a Japanese cherry (syn. *P.* 'Mount Fuji'). This is a spreading tree with large, white, fragrant flowers, and stunning orange-red autumn foliage.
ht 6m/20ft
sp 7.5m/25ft
Soil and position
Ordinary, fairly well-drained soil, preferably alkaline. May need support in exposed, windy areas.

Rhus typhina
STAGSHORN SUMACH

Stagshorn sumach produces spectacular orange-red leaf colour in autumn, and has velvety twigs with smooth bark. It throws up suckers to form a multi-stemmed tree or bush and takes happily to being pruned to size if required.
ht 3–4.5m/10–15ft
sp 3–4.5m/10–15ft
Can be cut to the ground each year in spring to produce vigorous new shoots and best foliage.
Soil and position
Will thrive in any soil that is not waterlogged. Best in a sunny position.
CAUTION: THE SAP CAN CAUSE SKIN BLISTERS.

Robinia pseudoacacia 'Frisia'
GOLDEN ACACIA
OR ROBINIA

A most ornamental foliage tree that makes a lovely backcloth for other garden plants, this acacia lookalike has stalks of small, paired leaflets, golden green in colour, which ripple in the breeze. Older trees have white pea-flowers which hang down in clusters in early summer. Robinias can be trained to grow against a wall and trimmed to size or grown as free-standing trees. Eventually, it must be admitted, they can grow rather large for a small garden.
ht 7.3m/24ft and eventually more
sp 3–4.5m/10–15ft
Soil and position
Any soil that does not get waterlogged, including alkaline soils, and full sun to light shade, as long as the tree is not exposed to harsh winds.

Sambucus racemosa 'Sutherland Gold'
GARDEN ELDER

This is an ornamental garden version of the common country elder and has upright, cone-shaped panicles of tiny whitish cream flowers in early summer, followed in late summer by heads of small, bright red berries. The abundant golden leaves have finely cut edges.

*ht and sp 3m/10ft but can be
trimmed to size*
Soil and position
Almost any soil in dappled shade.

Sorbus aria 'Lutescens'
WHITEBEAM

This is a shapely, smallish
whitebeam with silver-grey
young foliage, later turning grey-
green. The leaves flutter white in
the breeze because of the dense
white felt on their undersides.
In late spring the tree has light
and airy corymbs of small,
creamy white, fuzzy flowers
ht 9m/30ft
sp 7.5m/25ft
Soil and position
Ordinary, well-drained garden
soil in an open, sunny position.

Sorbus commixta
MOUNTAIN ASH

The mountain ash or rowan
makes a good specimen tree
with its pinnate leaves and white
spring flowers which develop
into firm round fruits in late
summer. Most also have good
autumn leaf colour. 'Embley' has
plentiful flowers followed by
bright red fruits. The glossy, dark
green leaves are particularly well-
shaped and put on an autumn
show of red and orange.
ht 10m/32ft
sp 7m/23ft
Soil and position
Well-drained but moist garden
soil and a position in sun or
semi-shade.
CAUTION: ALTHOUGH THE
FRUITS CAN BE USED FOR JAM
THEY CAUSE STOMACH UPSETS
IF EATEN RAW.

Spirea 'Arguta'
FOAM OF MAY
OR BRIDAL WREATH

This is a pretty and graceful
shrub; abundant white flowers
clothe the arching stems in late
spring and the stems themselves
have an appealing reddish tint

when bare from autumn to early
spring. *S. thunbergii* is rather
similar, and there are many other
spireas to choose, including the
(usually) pink-flowered *S. japonica*
which flowers in summer.
ht and sp to 2.5m/8ft; S. japonica
and S. thunbergii *are smaller*
Soil and position
Well-drained but reasonably
moist soil in sun or partial shade.

Symphoricarpos albus
'Laevigatus'
SNOWBERRY

Snowberries have to be chosen
carefully as they can colonize an
area, producing scrappy stems
and little fruit. However a good
snowberry is well worth
growing, especially for its effects
in winter. This one, with its large
white winter berries on delicate
stems is a good choice.
*ht and sp 1.8m/6ft but can be
kept trimmed*
Soil and position
Tolerates any soil except wet, and
any position from full sun to
shade.
CAUTION: THE BERRIES CAUSE
STOMACH UPSET IF EATEN AND
SOME PEOPLE FIND THEIR JUICE
IRRITATING TO THE SKIN.

Viburnum
VIBURNUM

There are so many viburnums
for the garden that this species
deserves several entries.
    Winter-flowering species,
with very fragrant pinkish white
flowers in small clusters on bare,
twiggy stems, are *Viburnum farreri*
(syn. *V. fragrans*), *V. grandiflorum*,
and *V. × bodnantense* 'Dawn', an
offspring of the two.
ht to 3m/10ft, sp to 2.5m/8ft
(Viburnum farreri);
ht and sp 1.8m/6ft (V.
grandiflorum);
ht 3m/10ft, sp 2m/6ft6in (V. ×
bodnantense 'Dawn')
    Viburnum × burkwoodii has
rounded balls of clustered

fragrant, white, tubular flowers
in spring.
ht and sp 2.5m/8ft
    Viburnum tinus is a robust,
evergreen viburnum that bears
white flowers, sometimes almost
continuously, from late autumn
till late spring.
ht to 3m/10ft, sp 1.8m/6ft
    Viburnum opulus, the guelder
rose, is a deciduous viburnum
with hydrangea-like heads of

▲ Sambucus racemosa *'Sutherland Gold'*.

creamy white flowers in late
spring, followed by jelly-red
berries in autumn.
ht to 3m/10ft
Soil and position
Fertile, fairly moist garden soil in
sun or semi-shade.
CAUTION: THE FRUITS OF
VIBURNUM OPULUS CAN CAUSE
STOMACH UPSETS IF EATEN.

index

PICTURE CREDITS:
Liz Eddison/Susanna Brown, Hampton Court 2000 45b/David Brum, Hampton Court 2000 26b, 44b; Designers: Butler Landscapes 38; Christopher Costin 45tr; Professor Masao Fukuhara 31b; Designer: Toby & Stephanie Hickish, Tatton Park 2000 16, 64b; Carol Klein 11bl; Designer: Lindsay Knight, Chelsea 2000 27r; Colin Luckett 37br; Natural & Oriental Water Gardens 29b, 31t; Angel Mainwaring 37bl, 35b; Alan Sargent 39b; David Squire 46; Wynniatt-Husey Clark 36. Neil Holmes 68b, 69t, b, 72, 80, 82, 83, 88tr, bl. Harry Smith Collection 77.